第3版
3rd Edition

"一带一路"篇
THE BELT AND ROAD INITIATIVE

中国关键词

KEYWORDS TO UNDERSTAND CHINA

权威解读当代中国

中国外文出版发行事业局(CICG)
当代中国与世界研究院(ACCWS)
中国翻译研究院(CATL)

新世界出版社
NEW WORLD PRESS

First Edition 2017
Second Edition 2019
Third Edition 2023

Compiled by
China International Communications Group
Academy of Contemporary China and World Studies
China Academy of Translation

Translated by
Han Qingyue and Cai Lijian

English text edited by
David W. Ferguson and Xu Mingqiang

Cover designed by
He Yuting

ISBN 978-7-5104-7745-4

Published by
NEW WORLD PRESS
24 Baiwanzhuang Street, Beijing 100037, China

Distributed by
NEW WORLD PRESS
24 Baiwanzhuang Street, Beijing 100037, China
Tel: 86-10-68995968
Fax: 86-10-68998705
Website: www.nwp.com.cn
E-mail: nwpcd@sina.com

Printed in the People's Republic of China

《中国关键词：“一带一路”篇》（第3版）编委会名单

Keywords to Understand China: The Belt and Road Initiative (3rd Edition)

Editorial Committee

前　言

源起两千多年前的古丝绸之路，凝聚了先辈们对美好生活的追求，促进了亚欧大陆各国互联互通，开启了人类文明史上的大交流时代。进入新世纪以来，面对全球性挑战，国际社会普遍呼唤和平、发展、合作、共赢。2013 年，习近平主席提出共建“一带一路”倡议，主张传承丝路精神，携手打造开放包容的国际合作平台，推动世界各国共同发展和繁荣。“一带一路”建设跨越不同地域、不同文明，顺应各国人民对共享发展机遇、创造美好生活的强烈愿望，有力推进全球互联互通，成为推动构建人类命运共同体的生动实践，受到国际社会普遍欢迎，在世界发展史上具有重要里程碑意义。

为讲好共建“一带一路”故事，增进外国受众对新时代中国对外开放和国际合作等相关内容的了解，“中国关键词”多语对外传播平台在《中国关键词：“一带一路”篇》（第 1 版、第 2 版）的基础上，修订更新了相关概念表述、案例数据等内容，推出《中国关键词：“一带一路”篇》（第 3 版），以期通过知识分享促进国际发展合作。本篇围绕共建“一带一路”的愿景与行动，选取 50 余个关键词进行简明扼要的介绍和解读，力图呈现这一倡议的基本概念和标志性内容，展现构建人类命运共同体的光明前景。本书为中外对照版，由于能力及时间所限，在中文词条遴选编写时，难免挂一漏万。同时，为使译文更符合目标语读者的阅读习惯，我们对翻译表达进行了创新探索，旨在提升读者的阅读体验。

“中国关键词”多语对外传播平台是中国外文出版发行事业局、当代中国与世界研究院和中国翻译研究院共同打造的国际传播品牌，主要围绕习近平新时代中国特色社会主义思想，进行中文词条专题编写、解读和多语种编译，通过平面、网络、移动端等多媒体、多渠道、多形态持续对外发布，旨在以外国受众易于阅读和理解的方式，阐释中国思想和中国道路，解读中国理念和中国方案。

讲故事需要关键词，讲好中国故事需要中国关键词。让我们用“中国关键词”点击中国、沟通世界，促进中外文明交流互鉴。

Introduction

Formed more than 2,000 years ago, the ancient Silk Road bore witness to how the people of the time yearned for a better life. It facilitated contacts between Asia and Europe and marked an era of extensive exchanges in human society.

In the new century, facing global challenges, the international community is in great need for peace, development, and cooperation for win-win results. In 2013, Chinese President Xi Jinping proposed the Belt and Road Initiative. He called on countries to carry forward the Silk Road spirit and join forces to create an international platform for open and inclusive cooperation to achieve common development and prosperity. The initiative accommodates various civilizations in different regions, responds to people's desire for a better life through sharing development opportunities, and represents a milestone in world history. It has been welcomed around the world as it has helped strengthen global connectivity, and serves as an example for building a global community of shared future.

To tell new stories about China's cooperation with other countries under the BRI framework and the country's progress in opening up in the new era, this booklet has been compiled based on the two previous editions (2017 and 2019). Readers will find latest updates and more cases of cooperation in this new edition. Through 52 keyword entries on the BRI, this concise introduction to basic concepts and concrete projects indicates that the prospects for a global community of shared future are bright.

Due to the scope of this work and its tight schedule, there may be oversights or inaccuracies in our selection of entries. To make the English version accessible to an international audience, the English editors have made alterations where they thought necessary, which might lead to inconsistencies between the Chinese and English texts.

The "China Keywords" multilingual platform is a brand of international communications undertaken by the China International Communications Group, the Academy of Contemporary China and World Studies and the China Academy of Translation. It offers expert interpretation of Xi Jinping Thought on Socialism with Chinese Characteristics for a New Era through multiple means of the media, and serves an international audience as a window into China's political thinking, policies, and approach to development.

Keywords are at the heart of any story. "China Keywords" are at the heart of the story of China. We hope that these "China Keywords" will help build a bridge of understanding between China and the rest of the world and promote exchanges between China and other civilizations.

Contents
目 录

基本概念
The Architecture

建设目标
Building Blocks

合作重点
Priority Areas of Cooperation

“走廊”建设

Economic Corridors

合作机制

Cooperation Mechanisms

合作案例
Projects Under Way

基本概念

The Architecture

“一带一路”

“一带一路”是“丝绸之路经济带”和“21世纪海上丝绸之路”的简称。2013年9月和10月，习近平出访中亚和东南亚时，分别提出了与相关国家共同建设“丝绸之路经济带”和“21世纪海上丝绸之路”的倡议。共建“一带一路”，是推动构建人类命运共同体的重要实践平台，是各方共同打造的全球公共产品。

“一带一路”倡议秉持“共商、共建、共享”原则，以实现“政策沟通、设施联通、贸易畅通、资金融通、民心相通”为主要内容，以打造“利益共同体、责任共同体、命运共同体”为目标，致力于将“一带一路”建成和平之路、繁荣之路、开放之路、创新之路、文明之路。

“一带一路”是发展的倡议、合作的倡议、开放的倡议，符合有关各方共同利益，顺应地区和全球合作潮流。“一带一路”建设由各方共同商量，成果由各方共同分享。倡议提出10年来，共建“一带一路”已吸引全球超过四分之三的国家和主要国际组织参与，联合国大会、联合国安理会

Belt and Road Initiative

The Belt and Road Initiative (BRI) – China's proposal to cooperate with other countries in building a Silk Road Economic Belt and a 21st Century Maritime Silk Road – was unveiled by Chinese President Xi Jinping during his visits to Central and Southeast Asia in September and October 2013. It is an important element of a global community of shared future and a global public good created through the concerted efforts of multiple parties.

The initiative focuses on policy coordination, infrastructure connectivity, unimpeded trade, financial integration, and closer people-to-people ties through honoring the principles of extensive consultation, joint contribution and shared benefits, and building a community of shared interests, of shared responsibility, and of shared future. The Belt and Road will become a road of peace, prosperity, opening up, and innovation that connects different civilizations.

An initiative for development, cooperation and opening up, the BRI reflects a convergence of interests and an increasing need for regional and global cooperation. BRI projects are agreed upon through joint consultation, and their benefits are shared by all. Over the past decade, more than three quarters of all countries and major international organizations have joined the initiative. The UN General

等也将“一带一路”建设相关内容纳入重要决议。共建“一带一路”从夯基垒台、立柱架梁到落地生根、持久发展，已成为开放包容、互利互惠、合作共赢的国际合作平台，受到国际社会普遍欢迎。

Assembly and Security Council have referenced the initiative in some of their resolutions.

First laying the foundations, then establishing sound frameworks, and ultimately taking root and reaping fruits, the BRI has grown into a platform for open and inclusive international cooperation to benefit all, which is welcomed by the international community.

丝绸之路经济带

2100多年前，中国汉代使者张骞两次出使西域，打开了中国同中亚友好交往的大门，开辟出一条横贯东西、连接欧亚的古丝绸之路。千百年来，中国同中亚各族人民一道推动了丝绸之路的兴起和繁荣，为世界文明交流交融、丰富发展作出了历史性贡献。

2013年9月，习近平在哈萨克斯坦纳扎尔巴耶夫大学发表演讲时提出，用创新的合作模式，共同建设“丝绸之路经济带”，进而以点带面、从线到片，逐步形成区域大合作。

丝绸之路沿线大部分国家处在亚太经济圈、欧洲经济圈这两个世界经济引擎的连接地带，整个区域经济发展曾长期存在“两边高、中间低”的现象，发展经济与追求美好生活是本地区国家与民众的普遍诉求。基于区域联通与协调发

Silk Road Economic Belt

The ancient Silk Road first emerged more than 2,100 years ago during the Han Dynasty, following the two westward journeys of Chinese envoy Zhang Qian (?-114 BC), which opened an overland route linking the East and the West, Asia and Europe. It also opened the door to friendly contacts between China and Central Asia. For two millennia, the people of China and Central Asia have expanded the Silk Road and maintained brisk exchanges through this route, making a historic contribution to the interaction, integration, enrichment and development of world civilizations.

In a speech at Kazakhstan's Nazarbayev University in September 2013, Xi Jinping proposed building a Silk Road Economic Belt to expand Eurasian economic cooperation. He advocated an innovative approach to cooperation, starting with individual projects to help spur larger-scale regional cooperative development.

Most of the countries along the ancient Silk Road are located in the region between the world's two economic engines: the Asia-Pacific economic circle and the European economic circle. Victims of long-term economic underdevelopment, people in these countries all desire rapid economic growth and a better life. Driven by the demand for regional connectivity and coordinated development,

展的需求，中国提出共建“丝绸之路经济带”倡议，就是在“古丝绸之路”概念基础上形成一个新的经济发展区域。这一区域横贯亚欧，总人口近30亿，具有独一无二的市场规模，被认为是“世界上最长、最具有发展潜力的经济大走廊”。

China created the idea of building a new economic belt along the ancient exchange route. With a huge market supported by a population of almost 3 billion, the proposed economic belt connects the Asia-Pacific region in the east and the developed European economies in the west. It is the longest economic corridor in the world, and potentially the most dynamic.

21世纪海上丝绸之路

海上丝绸之路是古代连接中国与世界其他地区的海上通道，自秦汉时期形成以来，一直是东西方经济、文化交流融通的重要桥梁。东南亚地区是海上丝绸之路的重要枢纽和组成部分。

2013年10月，习近平在印度尼西亚国会发表演讲时提出，共同建设21世纪海上丝绸之路，实现共同发展、共同繁荣。

21世纪海上丝绸之路的合作伙伴并不仅限于东盟，而是以点带线、以线带面，串起联通东盟、南亚、西亚、北非、欧洲等各大经济板块的市场链，发展面向南海、太平洋和印度洋的战略合作经济带。21世纪海上丝绸之路与丝绸之路经济带共同构成“一带一路”倡议。

21st Century Maritime Silk Road

As implied by its name, the ancient Maritime Silk Road refers to the centuries-old sea route that connected China and the rest of the world. Formed during the Qin and Han dynasties (221 BC-AD 220), this route played an important role in economic and cultural exchanges and integration between the East and the West. Southeast Asia was a nexus of this interaction.

Speaking to the Indonesian parliament in October 2013, Xi Jinping proposed jointly building a 21st Century Maritime Silk Road to boost development and common prosperity.

Starting with the launch of individual projects to help spur a wider range of cooperative activities, it envisions a network of interconnected markets linking ASEAN, South Asia, West Asia, North Africa and Europe, and a strategic partnership across the South China Sea and the Pacific and Indian oceans.

The Silk Road Economic Belt and the 21st Century Maritime Silk Road together make up the Belt and Road Initiative.

丝路精神

古丝绸之路是一条贸易之路，更是一条友谊之路，多民族、多种族、多宗教、多文化在此交汇融合，在长期交往过程中逐步形成了以“和平合作、开放包容、互学互鉴、互利共赢”为核心的丝路精神。这一精神，是欧亚各国在彼此交往中的经验积累和智慧总结，是人类文明的宝贵遗产，并已成为现代国际社会交往的一项基本原则。中国提出的“一带一路”倡议，就是对这一精神的传承和发扬，呼吁国际社会摒弃小圈子和零和博弈思维，在彼此尊重中共同发展、在求同存异中合作共赢。

2014年6月，习近平在中国—阿拉伯国家合作论坛第六届部长级会议开幕式上指出，千百年来，丝绸之路承载的和平合作、开放包容、互学互鉴、互利共赢精神薪火相传。

“和平合作”就是通过坦诚对话、深入沟通进行平等交流，不断深化不同国家和地区之间的交流合作，将政治关系优势、地缘毗邻优势、经济互补优势转化为务实合作优势、持续增长优势。“开放包容”就是以世界眼光和战略思维兼

Silk Road Spirit

The ancient Silk Road was a trade route of friendship where ethnic, racial, religious, and cultural convergence took place down the centuries. For millennia, interactions along this route shaped the Silk Road spirit – an expression of peace and cooperation, openness and inclusiveness, mutual learning, and mutual benefit.

This spirit is a valuable part of human heritage. It draws on the experience and wisdom accumulated in Eurasian interactions over the long course of history. It is also a fundamental support for international interaction today. Carrying on this spirit, the BRI calls for the international community to abandon exclusive blocs and zero-sum mentality, promote common development with mutual respect, and shelve differences in pursuit of win-win results.

Addressing the Sixth Ministerial Conference of the China-Arab States Cooperation Forum in June 2014, Xi Jinping hailed this spirit that has flourished through generations.

“Peace and cooperation” means increasing cooperation through frank dialogue and in-depth communication on an equal footing, and enabling healthy political relations, geographical proximity and economic complementarity to boost sustainable growth. “Openness and inclusiveness”

收并蓄、博采众长，这是丝路精神最显著的特征。“互学互鉴”就是在尊重文明多样性、道路多样化和发展水平不平衡等差异的基础上相互学习、相互借鉴，取长补短、共同提高。“互利共赢”就是不同种族、不同信仰、不同文化背景的国家和地区通过互惠合作，共同应对威胁和挑战，共同谋划利益和福祉，进而实现互惠互利的共赢发展。和平合作是前提，开放包容是根本，互学互鉴是手段，互利共赢是目的。

弘扬丝路精神，就是要促进文明互鉴，尊重道路选择，坚持合作共赢，倡导对话和平，推动“一带一路”共建国家共同发展，造福沿线各国人民。

means drawing on the strengths of others from a global perspective and with a strategic vision. This is the most salient feature of the spirit. "Mutual learning" means respecting the diversity of civilizations and development paths, recognizing imbalance in development, learning from each other in order to remedy shortcomings, and making progress together. "Mutual benefit" means that countries and regions with different races, beliefs and cultural backgrounds respond to threats and challenges through mutually beneficial cooperation so as to guarantee shared interests and common development.

Under the Silk Road spirit, countries can promote mutual learning among civilizations, respect each other's choice of path, increase cooperation for win-win results, and achieve peace through dialogue, to advance common development of the participating countries and benefit the people living along the Belt and Road routes.

丝路基金

2014年11月，习近平宣布，中国将出资400亿美元成立丝路基金。同年12月，丝路基金有限责任公司在北京注册成立。2017年5月，习近平在“一带一路”国际合作高峰论坛上提出，加大对“一带一路”建设资金支持，向丝路基金新增资金1000亿元人民币，鼓励金融机构开展人民币海外基金业务，规模预计约3000亿元人民币。

丝路基金秉承“开放包容、互利共赢”的理念，是中长期开发投资基金，重点为“一带一路”共建国家的基础设施建设、资源开发、产能合作和金融合作等有关项目提供投融资支持。它在现行国际经济金融秩序下运行，同其他全球和区域多边开发银行的关系是相互补充而非相互替代。丝路基金绝不是简单的经济援助，而是通过支持发展中国家互联互通建设，一方面为相关国家发展创造机遇，另一方面帮助他们增强自身发展能力，更好融入全球供应链、产业链、价值链。丝路基金面向亚洲域内外的投资者开放。

截至2023年6月底，丝路基金累计签约投资项目75

Silk Road Fund

The Silk Road Fund was established in Beijing in December 2014, following Xi Jinping's announcement in November that China would contribute US$40 billion for this purpose. He announced again at the Belt and Road Forum for International Cooperation in May 2017 that China would scale up financial support for the BRI by contributing an additional 100 billion yuan to the Silk Road Fund, and support financial institutions in conducting overseas Renminbi fund business to an estimated value of about 300 billion yuan.

The Silk Road Fund is a medium- and long-term fund for development investment. It supports infrastructure and resource development and industrial and financial cooperation in the countries along the land and sea Silk Roads. It operates under the current international economic and financial order and complements rather than replaces other global and regional multilateral development banks.

Instead of simply dispensing economic aid, the Fund, through improved connectivity, creates opportunities for BRI participants on the one hand, and helps them expand development capacity and join global supply, industrial and value chains on the other. It welcomes the participation of investors from Asia and beyond.

By the end of June 2023, the Fund had signed

个，承诺投资金额约220.4亿美元，初步探索形成符合“一带一路”建设实际、多元灵活且具自身特色的对外投融资模式。

agreements on 75 projects, with US$22 billion worth of promised investment, presenting a model of flexible, diverse investment adapted to the needs of the Belt and Road cooperation.

亚洲基础设施投资银行

亚洲基础设施投资银行（简称“亚投行”）是政府间性质的亚洲区域多边开发机构，也是全球首个由中国倡议设立的多边金融机构。亚投行重点支持基础设施建设，旨在促进亚洲区域的建设互联互通化和经济一体化进程，并且加强中国及其他亚洲国家和地区的合作。

2013年10月，习近平提出筹建亚投行的倡议。2015年12月，在历经800余天筹备后，由中国倡议成立、57国共同筹建的亚投行在北京成立。2018年12月，第73届联合国大会全会经协商一致通过决议，给予亚投行联合国大会永久观察员地位。

自2016年开业运营以来，亚投行成员不断增加。截至2022年年底，亚投行已拥有106个成员，覆盖全球81%的人口和65%的GDP，涵盖了联合国安理会常任理事国和二十国集团中的绝大多数成员国，成为成员数量仅次于世界银行的全球第二大国际多边开发机构，并连续获得相关国际评级机构给予的最高信用评级。

亚投行作为多边开发银行有其单独的业务标准，“一带一路”共建国家都可以获得亚投行的贷款，但应满足3个条

Asian Infrastructure Investment Bank

The Asian Infrastructure Investment Bank (AIIB) is a regional inter-governmental development institution and the first multinational financial institution initiated by China. Focusing on infrastructure investment, it is designed to improve connectivity and economic integration in Asia and reinforce cooperation between China and other Asian countries and regions.

Xi Jinping proposed the idea of creating the AIIB in October 2013. After more than 800 days of preparation by 57 countries, the AIIB was formally established in December 2015 in Beijing. In December 2018, the 73rd UN General Assembly adopted a resolution on granting the bank permanent observer status.

Since it opened in 2016, the bank has seen a growing membership. By the end of 2022, it had had 106 members representing 81 percent of the world's population and 65 percent of global GDP. These included most of the UN Security Council permanent members and most of the G20 members, making AIIB the world's second largest multilateral development institution with a membership next only to that of the World Bank. It has more than once been A-rated by major international credit rating agencies.

All BRI participating countries may apply for AIIB loans if their projects meet three criteria: The projects

件：一是融资的项目必须可实施可运营；二是项目必须是环保的；三是项目必须受到所在国的欢迎。亚投行初期投资重点领域包括能源与电力、交通和电信、农村和农业基础设施、供水与污水处理、环境保护、城市发展以及物流等。

亚投行的设立，有利于加快推进亚洲基础设施建设和互联互通建设，增强亚洲地区经济发展的内生动力，促进区域经济转型升级和经济稳定增长，加速亚洲经济一体化进程。截至2023年6月底，亚投行批准227个投资项目，共投资436亿美元，项目涉及交通、能源、公共卫生等领域，为推动“一带一路”建设、促进共同发展发挥重要作用。

must be financially viable, environmentally friendly, and welcomed by local communities. The bank initially invests in such sectors as energy and electricity, transport, telecommunications, rural and agricultural infrastructure, water supply and sewerage, environmental protection, urban development, and logistics.

The AIIB facilitates infrastructure construction and connectivity in Asia, increases Asia's driving force for economic development, promotes regional economic transformation, upgrading and stable growth, and advances economic integration. By the end of June 2023, the bank had provided US$43.6 billion for 227 projects in transport, energy, public health, and other fields. This gave a significant boost to BRI cooperation and common development.

推进“一带一路”建设工作领导小组

“一带一路”建设是一项宏大系统工程，仅在中国国内，其所涉及的政府机构、企业和社会组织就非常广泛，且很多建设项目周期长、任务重，需要专门的组织和领导机制，统筹各方做好共建工作。为此，中国政府专门成立了推进“一带一路”建设工作领导小组，负责审议“一带一路”建设工作的重大规划、政策、项目和相关具体问题，指导和协调落实“一带一路”合作倡议。外交部、商务部等是该小组的成员单位。该小组办公室设在国家发展和改革委员会，负责承担领导小组日常工作。此外，在中国的相关部委和省（自治区、直辖市）政府层面，均成立了推进“一带一路”建设工作领导小组，一般由相关部委和省（自治区、直辖市）主要领导担任负责人。

Steering Group for the Belt and Road Initiative

Implementing the Belt and Road Initiative is a massive undertaking. Domestically, it involves a wide range of government agencies, businesses and social organizations, and many projects are likely to extend over years. This calls for integrated planning and guidance.

A steering group for the BRI has been established at the state level to study important issues related to planning, policy, and projects, and to provide guidance and coordination in the implementation of the initiative. The group consists of representatives from government agencies such as the Ministry of Foreign Affairs and the Ministry of Commerce. The secretariat, which is placed under the National Development and Reform Commission, is responsible for the day-to-day work of the group.

Ministerial and provincial level steering groups have also been established, each headed by a key member of the leadership team of the ministry, or the province or equivalent administrative unit concerned.

《推动共建丝绸之路经济带和21世纪海上丝绸之路的愿景与行动》

2015年3月，国家发展和改革委员会、外交部、商务部联合发布《推动共建丝绸之路经济带和21世纪海上丝绸之路的愿景与行动》。这份文件阐明了“一带一路”倡议的时代背景、共建原则、框架思路、合作重点、合作机制、开放态势、积极行动、共建愿景等内容。文件强调，“一带一路”建设坚持共商、共建、共享原则，以实现“政策沟通、设施联通、贸易畅通、资金融通、民心相通”为主要内容，秉持和平合作、开放包容、互学互鉴、互利共赢的丝路精神，全方位推进务实合作，打造政治互信、经济融合、文化包容的利益共同体、命运共同体和责任共同体。此外，文件还介绍了中国各地区在“一带一路”建设中的角色定位。

Joining Hands to Build a Silk Road Economic Belt and a 21st Century Maritime Silk Road – Vision and Actions

In March 2015, a white paper entitled *Joining Hands to Build a Silk Road Economic Belt and a 21st Century Maritime Silk Road – Vision and Actions* was issued by China's National Development and Reform Commission, Ministry of Foreign Affairs, and Ministry of Commerce.

The document explained the background to the BRI, the guiding principles, broad objectives, priority areas, and mechanisms for cooperation. It also introduced the comparative strengths of different Chinese regions in opening up and the policies and actions China had carried out for early outcomes, and outlined the bright prospects for Belt and Road cooperation in the future. It emphasized the principles of extensive consultation, joint contribution, and shared benefits, and called for policy coordination, infrastructure connectivity, unimpeded trade, financial integration, and closer people-to-people ties. Also highlighted were the Silk Road spirit and the need to promote pragmatic cooperation across the board and build a community of shared interests, of shared responsibility and of shared future based on mutual political trust, economic integration and cultural inclusiveness. The white paper also illustrated the specific roles that different regions in China could play in implementing the initiative.

“五通”

2013年9月，习近平在哈萨克斯坦纳扎尔巴耶夫大学发表演讲，首次提出加强“政策沟通、道路联通、贸易畅通、货币流通、民心相通”，共同建设“丝绸之路经济带”的倡议。2015年3月，中国政府正式发布《推动共建丝绸之路经济带和21世纪海上丝绸之路的愿景与行动》，提出要以“政策沟通、设施联通、贸易畅通、资金融通、民心相通”（简称“五通”）为主要内容，打造“一带一路”沿线国家政治互信、经济融合、文化包容的利益共同体、责任共同体和命运共同体。

在“一带一路”建设全面推进过程中，“五通”既相互独立，在不同时间阶段各有重点，又是统一整体，需要相互促进、协同发展。随着共建“一带一路”高质量发展，中国同共建国家积极加强基础设施“硬联通”，持续完善互联互通合作；深化规则标准“软联通”，持续提高贸易投资自由

Five-Pronged Approach

In his speech at Kazakhstan's Nazarbayev University in September 2013, Xi Jinping proposed creating a Silk Road Economic Belt based on policy coordination, road connectivity, unimpeded trade, currency convertibility, and closer people-to-people ties.

In March 2015, China published the white paper entitled *Joining Hands to Build a Silk Road Economic Belt and a 21st Century Maritime Silk Road – Vision and Actions*. This document called for policy coordination, infrastructure connectivity, unimpeded trade, financial integration, and closer people-to-people ties – a five-pronged approach to the Belt and Road cooperation – in order to build a community of shared interests, of shared responsibility and of shared future on the basis of mutual political trust, economic integration and cultural inclusiveness.

While the five components of this approach are distinct from one another and will be more or less of a priority at different stages in building the Belt and Road, they are mutually reinforcing and form an integrated whole. Along with high-quality Belt and Road cooperation, China and other BRI participating countries will continue to strengthen "hard connectivity" in infrastructure, enhance "soft connectivity" through harmonized rules and standards to

化便利化水平；巩固人文交流“心联通”，不断促进共建国家人民相知相亲。

ensure trade and investment liberalization and facilitation, and forge stronger people-to-people bonds to build close friendships in participating countries.

建设目标
Building Blocks

利益共同体

共建“一带一路”是深受欢迎的国际公共产品和国际合作平台，涵盖世界上四分之三的国家和主要国际组织。“一带一路”贯穿亚欧非大陆，东牵发展势头强劲的东亚经济圈，西连发达的欧洲北美经济圈，有望建成世界跨度最大、最具活力的经济走廊，为各国政策对接、全球资源要素整合、促进世界和平和繁荣提供重要支撑。

受资源禀赋、产业基础、历史条件等因素的影响，“一带一路”共建国家之间发展不平衡，而且大部分为发展中国家，有着经济发展和民生建设的共同需求，各国结成休戚与共的利益共同体，开展互利合作的前景广阔。

推进“一带一路”建设，就是聚焦发展这个根本性问题，激发共建国家发挥比较优势，通过互联互通和贸易投资便利化等深度国际经济合作，将经济互补性转化为发展推动

Community of Shared Interests

Belt and Road cooperation is an international public good as well as an international cooperation platform, with the participation of three quarters of all countries and major international organizations.

Spanning three continents – Asia, Europe and Africa, Belt and Road cooperation is expected to create the world's most expansive and most dynamic economic corridor, with the vibrant East Asia at one end and the developed economies of Europe and North America at the other. It will help align the policies of different countries, integrate global resource factors, and promote world peace and prosperity.

Limited by natural resources, industrial conditions, and historical experience, most of the BRI participating countries are still developing countries at different stages and with similar needs for economic development and wellbeing improvement. This offers good prospects for their building a community of shared interests through mutually beneficial cooperation.

Belt and Road cooperation, above all, helps solve the focal task of development. The participating countries can exploit their comparative strengths, and their close cooperation to strengthen connectivity and liberalize and facilitate trade and investment will turn economic complementarity into new drivers to tackle such problems

力，着力解决发展失衡、治理困境、数字鸿沟、分配差距等问题，建设开放、包容、普惠、平衡、共赢的经济全球化，从而实现互利共赢。

as imbalance in development, governance difficulties, and digital and income gaps. This will help make economic globalization more open, inclusive, balanced and beneficial for all.

责任共同体

“一带一路”建设秉持共商、共建、共享原则，不是封闭的，而是开放包容的。“一带一路”倡议由中国提出，需要沿线国家和相关国家共同参与建设。

在推动落实倡议的过程中，相关各方会有不同侧重的利益考虑，也会遇到各种难以预料的问题，这就需要各方集思广益，携手应对挑战，合力化解威胁，共同承担责任。由于各国参与的深度和方式有所不同，承担的责任也不尽相同。作为倡议方，中国诚心诚意对待沿线国家，做到言必信、行必果，承担起应尽的责任。

Community of Shared Responsibility

Belt and Road cooperation follows the principles of extensive consultation, joint contribution, and shared benefits. The cooperation is not isolated, but open and inclusive. While the BRI is an initiative proposed by China, the participation of countries along the proposed routes and other related countries is indispensable to its implementation.

Divergent national interests and priorities, as well as unforeseen events, could present a serious challenge. Broad-based consultation is therefore essential. Only through joint efforts and shared responsibility can any threat to progress be neutralized. From this perspective, it is agreed that responsibilities could vary depending on different levels of participation.

As the sponsor, China is ready and willing to act in good faith toward its partners, honor its commitments, and fulfill its responsibilities.

命运共同体

2013年3月，习近平在莫斯科国际关系学院发表演讲，首次在国际场合向世界提出“命运共同体”理念，这是进入新时代以来中国就人类未来发展提出的方案。“命运共同体”强调整体思维，推崇共生共荣的关系，谋求持久和平与共同繁荣。

一个国家的命运要掌握在本国人民手中，世界的前途命运必须由各国共同掌握，各国在追求本国利益时兼顾别国利益，在追求自身发展时兼顾别国发展。“一带一路”建设体现的正是这种“命运共同体”理念。通过“一带一路”推动构建命运共同体，需要建立在利益共同体和责任共同体的基础之上。一方面，各国要在经贸和投资领域不断扩大利益交汇点，把经济互补性转化为发展推动力；另一方面，各国需要共同担负解决国际性难题的责任，共同打造互利共赢的合作架构。

Community of Shared Future

In his speech at the Moscow State Institute of International Relations in March 2013, Xi Jinping for the first time introduced to the international audience the concept of a global community of shared future. This is China's proposal for human development with the country entering a new era. It emphasizes the virtue of holistic thinking, cosmopolitan ideals, and the pursuit of lasting peace and shared prosperity.

The destiny of a country should be in the hands of its people, and the future of the world must be shaped jointly by the people of the world. A country's interests should be pursued with other countries' interests in mind. The implementation of any national development strategy should be accompanied by due consideration of the development needs of others.

Underlying the BRI is the understanding that we all share one world. Under the BRI, a community of shared future can be built only on the basis of shared interests and shared responsibility. Sustained efforts should thus be made to expand cooperation in trade and investment, where convergence of interests occurs, and to transform economic complementarity into new drivers of development. At the same time, all countries should join forces in dealing with international challenges and building a cooperative framework that benefits all.

绿色丝绸之路

气候和环境问题是人类社会面临的共同问题，也是“一带一路”建设面临的现实问题。2016年6月，习近平在乌兹别克斯坦最高会议立法院发表演讲时提出，要着力深化环保合作，践行绿色发展理念，加大生态环境保护力度，携手打造“绿色丝绸之路”。此前中国发布的《推动共建丝绸之路经济带和21世纪海上丝绸之路的愿景与行动》也明确提出，强化基础设施绿色低碳化建设和运营管理，在建设中充分考虑气候变化影响，在投资贸易中突出生态文明理念，加强生态环境、生物多样性和应对气候变化合作，共建绿色丝绸之路。2022年3月发布的《关于推进共建“一带一路”绿色发展的意见》作为中国政府在绿色丝绸之路建设方面的顶层设

Silk Road of Green Development

Climate change and environmental protection are common concerns of humanity. They are also problems afflicting the Belt and Road cooperation.

Addressing the Legislative Chamber of the Uzbek Supreme Assembly in June 2016, Xi Jinping emphasized the need to strengthen cooperation in environmental and ecological protection, in order to build a Silk Road of green development.

This idea had previously been affirmed by the Chinese government in the white paper *Joining Hands to Build a Silk Road Economic Belt and a 21st Century Maritime Silk Road – Vision and Actions*. The document highlighted the importance of a green, low-carbon approach to building and operating infrastructure, taking into full account the imperative to mitigate the impact of climate change. It encouraged joint efforts to build a Silk Road of green development by integrating ecological and environmental considerations into trade and investment strategies and expanding cooperation in protecting the environment and biodiversity and addressing climate change.

The Guidelines on Promoting Green Development in Belt and Road Cooperation, issued in March 2022, presented the top-level design of the Chinese government for building a Silk Road of green development. The

计，围绕推进绿色发展重点领域合作、推进境外项目绿色发展、完善绿色发展支撑保障体系，提出了15项具体任务。

绿色丝绸之路体现了可持续发展的理念，它要求在“一带一路”建设中秉承绿色发展和环境保护理念，注重经济社会发展与生态环境保护相协调，坚持共同但有区别的责任原则和各自能力原则，充分尊重共建国家实际，建设更紧密的绿色发展伙伴关系，共享绿色发展成果。建设绿色丝绸之路是积极应对气候变化、维护全球生态安全的重大举措，是推进共建“一带一路”高质量发展、构建人与自然生命共同体的重要载体。

document set 15 tasks for increasing cooperation in the key fields, advancing overseas projects, and building sound supporting systems to boost green development.

Contributing to the goal of sustainable development and informed by the concept of environmentally friendly development, the initiative for building a Silk Road of green development calls for a balance between socio-economic development and environmental protection. It upholds the principles of common but differentiated responsibilities and of respective capabilities and respects the conditions of individual countries as they are building closer partnerships in pursuing green development that benefits all. Building a Silk Road of green development is a significant move to address climate change and safeguard global ecological security. It is an important means to promote high-quality Belt and Road cooperation and build a community of life formed by humans and nature.

健康丝绸之路

健康是发展的核心，是人类的共同追求。推进全球卫生事业，是落实2030年可持续发展议程的重要组成部分。2016年6月，习近平在乌兹别克斯坦最高会议立法院发表演讲时提议，着力深化医疗卫生合作，加强在传染病疫情通报、疾病防控、医疗救援、传统医药领域互利合作，携手打造“健康丝绸之路”。2017年1月，中国政府与世界卫生组织签署了双方关于“一带一路”卫生领域合作的谅解备忘录。

健康是“一带一路”倡议中社会认同度很高的合作领域，也是各国民心相通的重要纽带。健康丝绸之路的主要目标是提高“一带一路”沿线国家整体的健康卫生水平。新冠肺炎疫情的发生再次表明，人类是一个休戚与共的命运共同体。中国基于人类命运共同体理念，呼吁打造健康丝绸之路，并进一步提出构建人类卫生健康共同体，对于强化全球战疫信心、加强协调与合作具有重要引领作用。中国因时因

Silk Road of Health Cooperation

Health is a core development issue and a shared concern of humanity. Promoting health at a global level is an important component of the 2030 Agenda for Sustainable Development.

In his speech to the Legislative Chamber of the Uzbek Supreme Assembly in June 2016, Xi Jinping proposed building a Silk Road of health cooperation by strengthening information-sharing on communicable diseases and cooperation on disease prevention and control, medical relief and assistance, and traditional medicine. In January 2017, the Chinese government and the World Health Organization signed a memorandum of understanding to this end.

Cooperation on health enjoys strong public support as it responds to the needs of the people of all countries. The initiative for building a Silk Road of health cooperation aims to improve public health in the countries along the Belt and Road. The fight against Covid-19 proves that humanity is a closely connected community. Based on the vision of a global community of shared future, China has called for building a Silk Road of health cooperation and a global community of health for all. This has boosted world confidence in the fight against the virus and helped strengthen coordination and cooperation. China has

势优化调整防控政策措施，高效统筹疫情防控和经济社会发展，积极开展全球抗疫合作，以务实行动推进健康丝绸之路建设和全球公共卫生合作，为增进各国民众健康福祉作出重要贡献。

made timely adjustments to its virus-control policies and measures and succeeded in balancing epidemic control and socio-economic development. It has also participated in global anti-Covid-19 cooperation, and promoted progress in building a Silk Road of health cooperation and in global public health programs, contributing to the health improvement in relevant countries.

智力丝绸之路

共建“一带一路”既是中国提出的倡议，也是沿线国家的共同愿景。实现这样的愿景，既需要各方的诚意和决心，也需要各方的远见卓识。2016年6月，习近平在华沙出席丝路国际论坛时提出，智力先行，强化智库的支撑引领作用。加强对“一带一路”建设方案和路径的研究，在规划对接、政策协调、机制设计上做好政府的参谋和助手，在理念传播、政策解读、民意通达上做好桥梁和纽带。随后，习近平在乌兹别克斯坦最高会议立法院发表演讲时进一步提出，中方倡议成立“一带一路”职业技术合作联盟，培养培训各类专业人才，携手打造“智力丝绸之路”。

在共建“一带一路”高质量发展阶段，各方会面临很多新形势、新问题、新挑战，需要越来越多的智力和人才支持，需要各方相互学习、取长补短，共同提出解决方案。当

Silk Road of Intellectual Cooperation

The BRI proposed by China is also a shared vision of the countries along the Belt and Road routes. Sincerity, resolution and far-sighted actions are needed from all sides to make the vision a reality.

At the Silk Road Forum in Warsaw in June 2016, Xi Jinping emphasized the importance of intellectual endeavors and the supporting role of think tanks in leading the way. Organizations such as think tanks need to research the means to promote the initiative and the courses of action needed, acting as consultants to government decision-making with regard to planning alignment, policy coordination, and institutional design. They can also help disseminate information about the guiding principles of the initiative, interpret relevant policies, and express public views.

When addressing the Legislative Chamber of the Uzbek Supreme Assembly, also held in June 2016, Xi proposed the establishment of a technical cooperation alliance under the BRI to develop talent and build a Silk Road of intellectual cooperation.

Worthwhile progress in implementing the initiative will reveal new challenges. Overcoming these challenges requires brainpower and expertise. It is therefore vital for countries to learn from each other and cooperate to look for

前，“一带一路”共建国家不同程度地存在人才短缺、高智力投入不足等问题，而智力丝绸之路的主要目标正是推进沿线国家的人才培养和智力交流。

solutions. The Silk Road of intellectual cooperation aims to develop talent and boost exchanges of expertise in response to the shortfalls in skilled personnel and intellectual support in participating countries.

和平丝绸之路

“一带一路”沿线，尤其是丝绸之路经济带沿线，面临较为严重的恐怖主义、分裂主义和极端主义威胁，部分国家之间的关系较为紧张，时常伴有局部冲突，也有部分国家内部政局不稳。因此，破解地区动荡局势，维护地区和平稳定，对于“一带一路”建设至关重要。2016年6月，习近平在乌兹别克斯坦最高会议立法院发表演讲时提出，着力深化安保合作，践行共同、综合、合作、可持续的亚洲安全观，推动构建具有亚洲特色的安全治理模式，携手打造“和平丝绸之路”。

和平丝绸之路包含两个基本内涵：一是“一带一路”建设必须在相对和平的环境里进行；二是“一带一路”建设能促进地区和平稳定。以发展促和平促安全，这是中国提出的思路，也是被实践证明很有成效的办法。

Silk Road of Peace

Serious terrorist, secessionist and extremist threats lurk along the Belt and Road, especially along the Belt. There is also tension between some of the countries along the routes, giving rise to occasional localized conflicts. Furthermore, a number of countries are subject to internal instability. For Belt and Road cooperation to proceed, it is essential to defuse turmoil and maintain peace and stability at the regional level.

In his speech to the Legislative Chamber of the Uzbek Supreme Assembly in June 2016, Xi Jinping called for greater cooperation on security. It is critical, he said, to promote a new Asian security concept that emphasizes joint and comprehensive measures and cooperation in ensuring sustainable security, and to create a security governance framework with Asian characteristics – in sum, to jointly build a Silk Road of peace.

A Silk Road of peace has two implications: An environment of relative stability is indispensable for the BRI to thrive, and Belt and Road cooperation contributes to regional peace and stability. China believes that development promotes peace and security, a conviction that has been borne out by experience.

数字丝绸之路

数字丝绸之路是数字经济发展和“一带一路”倡议的结合，体现了数字技术对“一带一路”倡议的支撑。2017年5月，习近平在首届“一带一路”国际合作高峰论坛上提出，要坚持创新驱动发展，加强在数字经济、人工智能、纳米技术、量子计算机等前沿领域合作，推动大数据、云计算、智慧城市建设，连接成21世纪的数字丝绸之路。2019年4月，习近平在第二届“一带一路”国际合作高峰论坛上进一步提出，共同把握数字化、网络化、智能化发展机遇，共同探索新技术、新业态、新模式，探寻新的增长动能和发展路径，建设数字丝绸之路、创新丝绸之路。

数字技术发轫于互联网的发展，其缘起就是为了更好的连接，特征就是去中心化。平等、开放、信任、共享是数字经济的基因，这与和平合作、开放包容、互学互鉴、互利共赢的丝路精神相通。数字丝绸之路的内涵就是以平等为基

Digital Silk Road

A digital Silk Road integrates the digital economy and the BRI, which has to be backed by digital technology.

Speaking at the opening of the First Belt and Road Forum for International Cooperation in May 2017, Xi Jinping called for innovation-driven development and closer cooperation in frontier areas such as the digital economy, artificial intelligence, nanotechnology, and quantum computing, and advancing the development of big data, cloud computing and smart cities, to build a digital Silk Road in the 21st century.

At the opening of the Second Belt and Road Forum for International Cooperation in April 2019, he recommended that all countries seize opportunities created by digital, networked and smart development, explore new technologies and new forms and models of business, foster new growth drivers, explore new development pathways, and build a digital Silk Road and a Silk Road of innovation.

Digital technology was created based on the internet, for the simple purpose of better connectivity. Decentralization is what it is all about. Equality, openness, trust and sharing are the essential components of the digital economy. This coincides with the essence of the Silk Road spirit – peaceful cooperation, openness and inclusiveness, mutual learning, and mutual benefit. The digital Silk Road will be built

础、以开放为特征、以信任为路径、以共享为目标，推动数字互联互通，弥合“数字鸿沟”，加快相关国家经济社会发展。

around sharing based on equality, openness, and trust to narrow the digital gap and accelerate the socio-economic development of participating countries.

信息丝绸之路

共建“一带一路”需要各国在信息交流上互联互通，而互联互通重在通信和网络先行。信息丝绸之路，就是各国信息基础设施的互联互通，同时涉及信息化建设、信息产业、网络传播、网络治理、媒体交流等合作内容。2015年3月发布的《推动共建丝绸之路经济带和21世纪海上丝绸之路的愿景与行动》明确提出，共同推进跨境光缆等通信干线网络建设，提高国际通信互联互通水平，畅通信息丝绸之路。

信息丝绸之路是传统丝绸之路的发展和创新，不仅包括“一带一路”信息化建设，实现相关国家在数据信息服务、互联网业务、国际通信业务领域的互联互通，还涵盖媒体合作和信息共享，以信息畅通带动资金流动、商品流通和人文交流。

Information Silk Road

To make Belt and Road cooperation effective, countries have to connect with each other and exchange information, and this calls for connectivity of communications and networks. An information Silk Road will link up the information infrastructure facilities in different countries, and this involves information technology, the information industry, online communication, cyberspace governance, and media exchanges.

It was stated in the white paper *Joining Hands to Build a Silk Road Economic Belt and a 21st Century Maritime Silk Road – Vision and Actions* that countries should work together to create cross-border optical cables and other communications trunk line networks, improve international communications connectivity, and create an information Silk Road.

An information Silk Road is a further innovative development of the traditional Silk Road. In addition to informationization, connectivity must be achieved in data information services, internet services, and international communications services, as well as in media cooperation and information sharing, so as to guide the flow of capital and goods and cultural and people-to-people exchanges with smooth information flows.

空中丝绸之路

2017年6月，习近平在会见卢森堡首相贝泰尔时明确提出，要深化双方在“一带一路”建设框架内金融和产能等合作，中方支持建设郑州—卢森堡“空中丝绸之路”。2022年5月发布的《“十四五”时期推进“空中丝绸之路”建设高质量发展实施方案》进一步明确，更好满足与共建国家互联互通，构建安全可靠、便捷高效、绿色集约、互惠包容的“空中丝绸之路”。

“空中丝绸之路”是中国建设“一带一路”倡议的重要有机组成部分。近年来，郑州—卢森堡“空中丝绸之路”搭建了中欧互联互通的空中桥梁，构建了以郑州为亚太枢纽、卢森堡为欧美枢纽、基本覆盖全球主要经济体的航线网络，促进东亚经济圈和欧洲经济圈融合发展，吸引更多国家参与“一带一路”建设。

Silk Road in the Air

When meeting with visiting Luxembourg's Prime Minister Xavier Bettel in June 2017, Xi Jinping said that the two countries should expand cooperation in finance and industrial capacity under the BRI framework, and that China would support building a Silk Road in the air between Zhengzhou in China and Luxembourg in Europe. According to the Plan on Building a High-quality Silk Road in the Air during the 14th Five-year Plan Period, released in May 2022, China will improve connectivity with BRI participating countries and build a Silk Road in the air that is safe, reliable, convenient, green, and beneficial to all.

The Silk Road in the air is an important component of Belt and Road cooperation. The Zhengzhou-Luxembourg link serves as an air bridge between China and Europe, and joins a network of flights reaching the main economies, with Zhengzhou as the hub in the Asia-Pacific region and Luxembourg as the hub in the European and American regions. This has boosted the integrated development of the two economic circles in East Asia and Europe and given other countries a greater incentive to join Belt and Road cooperation.

合作重点

Priority Areas of Cooperation

政策沟通

政策沟通是“一带一路”建设的重要保障。政策沟通，就是共建国家和国际组织在深化利益融合、促进政治互信并达成合作共识的前提下，本着友好对话、求同存异的原则，建立多层次政府间政策沟通机制，就经济发展战略和对策进行充分交流对接，共同制定推进区域合作的规划和措施，协商解决合作中的问题，共同为务实合作及大型项目实施提供政策支持，从而形成趋向一致的战略、决策、政策和规则，结成更为巩固的命运共同体。

做好政策沟通，需要各方加强发展战略对接、发展规划对接、机制和平台对接、具体项目对接，实现规划衔接、发展融合、利益共享的目标。

Policy Coordination

Policy coordination is key to effective implementation of the BRI. In order to expand shared interests, build mutual political trust, and ensure consensus on further cooperation, it is important for the participating countries and international organizations to engage in friendly dialogue, seeking common ground while shelving differences, and building multilevel mechanisms for inter-governmental communication on economic development strategies and policies. This will help them work out plans and measures for regional cooperation, discuss the solutions to cooperation-related problems, and provide policy support to pragmatic approaches and large projects. This will also help them harmonize strategies, decision-making processes, policies, and rules, for building a closer community of shared future.

Policy coordination requires all parties to actively synergize their development strategies, plans, mechanisms, platforms, and projects for integrated development and shared interests.

设施联通

设施互联互通是“一带一路”建设的优先领域。设施联通，就是在尊重相关国家主权和安全关切的基础上，推动共建国家加强基础设施建设规划、技术标准体系的对接，共同推进国际骨干通道建设，逐步形成连接亚洲各次区域以及亚欧非之间的基础设施网络。设施联通既包括传统的公路、铁路、航空、航运、管道等的联通，也包括电力、电信、邮政、边防、海关和质检、规划等新领域的联通，从而将活跃的东亚经济圈、发达的欧洲经济圈和经济发展潜力巨大的中间广大腹地国家结成携手发展的利益共同体。

做好设施联通，需要推动陆上、海上、天上、网上“四位一体”的联通，聚焦关键通道、关键城市、关键项目，联结陆上公路、铁路网络和海上港口网络。同时，还应注

Infrastructure Connectivity

Infrastructure connectivity is a priority area under the BRI. While respect for each other's sovereignty and security concerns is indispensable, a closer alignment of infrastructure development plans and technical standards is called for between the participating countries. This will facilitate the construction of key international arteries and build an infrastructure network that not only links all the subregions in Asia but also extends out to Europe and Africa.

The new concept of connectivity is not confined to traditional channels such as highways, railways, aviation routes, shipping routes, and pipelines. It also covers such areas as power supplies, telecommunications, postal services, border controls, customs, quality controls, and planning. Efforts to improve connectivity aim to link the vibrant East Asia with the developed economies in Europe and a host of other countries in between with huge potential for economic development. With interests interlocked, all countries concerned are encouraged to seek cooperation in pursuit of shared prosperity.

Infrastructure connectivity means connectivity on land and sea, in the air, and on the internet, which will link up all the key channels, major cities, significant projects, and networks of highways, railways and seaports. Also essential

重基础设施的绿色低碳化建设和运营管理，充分考虑气候变化影响。

is the green and low-carbon approach to building and operating infrastructure, taking into full account the impact of climate change.

贸易畅通

贸易畅通是“一带一路”建设的重点内容。贸易畅通，就是为国际贸易往来提供最大程度的便利，消除经贸壁垒，促进贸易增长，加强投资合作，推动包容和可持续发展，让共建国家在合作中更多获益，共享经济全球化红利。

做好贸易畅通，需要共同建设自由贸易网络体系，促进贸易和投资便利化；需要共同商建自由贸易区，构建区域内和各国良好的营商环境；需要共同提高技术性贸易措施透明度，降低非关税壁垒；需要共同拓宽贸易领域，优化贸易结构，挖掘贸易新增长点，促进贸易平衡；需要以投资带动贸易发展，加强生态环境、生物多样性和应对气候变化合作，共建绿色丝绸之路；需要共同优化产业链、价值链、供应链和服务链，促进沿线国家和地区产业互补、互动与互助；需

Unimpeded Trade

Removing barriers to trade is a major task in building the Belt and Road and keeping international trade expanding and investment growing, which will promote inclusive and sustainable development in the participating countries and bring them more benefits from economic globalization.

Major measures may include:

– creating free trade networks to facilitate trade and investment;

– opening free trade areas to create a business-friendly environment at regional and national levels;

– improving the transparency of technical trade measures and reducing non-tariff barriers;

– expanding the sectors of trade, improving trade structures, and exploring new growth areas to attain trade balance;

– boosting trade with investment, and increasing cooperation on eco-environmental and bio-diversity protection and response to climate change to build a Silk Road of green development;

– optimizing the industrial, value, supply and service chains, and promoting economic complementarity, interaction, and mutual assistance between countries and regions concerned;

– exploring new development opportunities and

要共同探索新的开放开发之路，形成互利共赢、多元平衡、安全高效的开放型经济体系。

creating an open economic environment that encourages the search for win-win solutions, respects diversity, and ensures security and efficiency.

资金融通

资金融通是“一带一路”建设的重要支撑。资金融通，就是各方加强金融合作，推动构建长期、稳定、可持续、风险可控的多元化融资体系，为“一带一路”高质量发展提供金融支撑。

做好资金融通，需要深化金融合作，推进亚洲货币稳定体系、投融资体系和信用体系建设，通过提供更多惠及各方的公共金融产品，推动金融系统化；需要发挥亚洲基础设施投资银行、金砖国家新开发银行、丝路基金等机构及各国主权基金在“一带一路”重点项目建设中的金融服务和资金引导作用；需要扩大沿线国家双边本币结算和货币互换的范围和规模，推动亚洲债券市场开放发展，为互联互通提供持续保障；需要深化多边金融合作，深化银行联合体务实合作，引导商业股权投资基金和社会资金参与共建；需要加强金融

Financial Integration

Financial integration is an important support for the BRI. All parties involved should increase their financial cooperation and work together to build a long-term diversified fund-raising system that is stable and sustainable and keeps risks under control, to provide financial support for high-quality Belt and Road cooperation.

Key measures may include:

– increasing financial cooperation to ensure currency stability and build a sound framework for investment, financing and credit services in Asia, and expanding the availability of public financial products;

– strengthening the role of the Asian Infrastructure Investment Bank, the BRICS New Development Bank, the Silk Road Fund, and the sovereign wealth funds of the countries concerned, in funding key projects and guiding investment;

– expanding local currency settlement for bilateral trade and currency swaps, and promoting the opening up and development of bond markets in Asia to provide continuous support to connectivity;

– facilitating multilateral financial cooperation, giving full play to inter-bank consortiums, and encouraging equity investment funds and private capital to invest;

– strengthening cooperation on financial regulation,

监管合作，完善风险应对和危机处置的制度安排，构建区域性金融风险预警系统，形成应对跨境风险和危机处置的交流合作机制。

improving risk response and crisis management mechanisms, and building regional financial risk early-warning systems, to address any cross-border risks and crises.

民心相通

民心相通是“一带一路”建设的社会根基。作为沟通多元文化和众多国家的重大倡议和重要平台，“一带一路”能否成功，从根本上取决于民心能否相通，直接体现在沿线国家人民的获得感、认可度和参与度上。民心相通，就是各国弘扬丝路精神，在科学、教育、文化、旅游、卫生、民间交往等各领域广泛开展合作，为“一带一路”建设夯实民意基础，筑牢社会根基。民心相通不仅包括人文交流，还强调在交流的基础上保持尊重，在尊重的基础上建立理解，在理解的基础上达成共识。

做好民心相通，需要加强民生合作，开展惠民工程，改善共建国家人民生活，增进民生福祉；需要加强各国政党、议会、民间组织的往来，深化智库、媒体、高校、企业、科研机构、社会组织等交流合作，汇聚各方智慧，促进互学互鉴；需要深化各领域人力资源开发合作，支持专业技术人才培养，提高各国经济社会发展的内生动力。

Closer People-to-People Ties

People-to-people ties provide an anchor for the BRI. Without such an anchor, the BRI goal of connecting diverse cultures and different countries would be out of reach. The local people's sense of gain and their recognition and participation are therefore indispensable to the initiative's success.

To this end, countries must lay solid foundations for the BRI by carrying on the Silk Road spirit and conducting extensive cooperation in science, education, culture, tourism, health and non-governmental exchanges. In addition to cultural and people-to-people exchanges, mutual respect and mutual understanding are the basis for building consensus.

Specific measures may include:

– increasing cooperation on wellbeing projects to improve the lives of the people in participating countries;

– expanding exchanges among political parties, parliaments, non-governmental organizations, think tanks, the media, universities, enterprises, research institutions, and social organizations to pool wisdom through mutual learning;

– encouraging collaboration among human resources in various fields and supporting the training of specialists so as to increase the internal driving force for economic and social development of the countries concerned.

“走廊”建设

Economic Corridors

中蒙俄经济走廊

2014年9月，习近平在首次中蒙俄三国元首会晤时提出，将丝绸之路经济带同俄罗斯跨欧亚大铁路、蒙古国草原之路倡议对接，打造中蒙俄经济走廊的倡议。2016年6月，三国签署《建设中蒙俄经济走廊规划纲要》，标志着“一带一路”首个多边经济合作走廊正式实施。

中蒙俄经济走廊是丝绸之路经济带的重要组成部分，其中短期目标是增加三方贸易量、提升产品竞争力、加强过境运输便利化、发展基础设施，长期目标是建设和拓展互利共赢的经济发展空间，提升三方在国际市场上的联合竞争力，实现共同繁荣的愿景。

中蒙俄经济走廊有2条主线路：一是从京津冀到呼和浩特，再到蒙古国和俄罗斯；二是由大连、沈阳、长春、哈尔滨到满洲里，再到俄罗斯赤塔。该走廊重点关注七大合作领域，即促进交通基础设施发展及互联互通、加强口岸建设和

China-Mongolia-Russia Economic Corridor

The idea of the China-Mongolia-Russia Economic Corridor (CMREC) was proposed by Xi Jinping in September 2014 during the first trilateral meeting of the three heads of state. The CMREC aims to align the Silk Road Economic Belt with Russia's transcontinental rail plan and Mongolia's Steppe Road program. In June 2016, the three countries signed a development plan based on the proposal, marking the formal implementation of the first multilateral economic corridor under the BRI.

As an important component of the Silk Road Economic Belt, the CMREC is expected to increase trilateral trade volume, increase product competitiveness, facilitate cross-border transport, and build infrastructure in the near future. The long-term goal is to expand development opportunities beneficial to all and increase trilateral collective competitiveness in the international market.

The CMREC has two key traffic arteries. One extends from China's Beijing-Tianjin-Hebei region to Hohhot and on to Mongolia and Russia; the other extends from China's Dalian, Shenyang, Changchun, Harbin and Manzhouli to Russia's Chita.

Seven major areas of cooperation are envisaged: transport infrastructure and connectivity; port construction, and customs and border inspection and quarantine services;

海关及检验检疫监管、加强产能与投资合作、深化经贸合作、拓展人文交流合作、加强生态环保合作、推动地方及边境地区合作。

近年来，三方以中蒙俄经济走廊建设为契机，在基础设施联通方面，持续加大铁路、公路、口岸、航空等领域合作对接力度，初步形成了以铁路、公路和边境口岸为主体的跨国基础设施联通网络。2022年12月下旬，作为中蒙唯一铁路口岸的二连浩特铁路口岸扩能改造工程全部竣工，铁路口岸宽准轨接发列车线路增加到30条，货物接运能力提升20%。在贸易畅通方面，三方打造开放合作平台，采取贸易便利化措施，使贸易规模稳中有升。目前，中国已成为俄罗斯和蒙古国的最大贸易伙伴国。

推进中蒙俄经济走廊建设，优先推进三国毗邻地区次区域合作，充分发挥各地比较优势，将进一步拉动多边投资和贸易大幅增长，有力促进教育、科技、旅游等人文交流，带动境外合作区建设稳步推进，为其他地区区域经济合作提供良好范本。

industrial capacity and investment; trade; cultural and people-to-people exchanges; environmental protection; cooperation in the adjacent border regions.

Thanks to the three countries' ongoing cooperation in recent years, a cross-border infrastructure network consisting mainly of railways, highways and border ports has taken shape. With the completion of the expansion of the Erenhot railway port, the only rail port between China and Mongolia, in late December 2022, the train lines connecting both wide gauge and standard gauge increased to 30, and the cargo transport capacity was thus expanded by 20 percent. In terms of unimpeded trade, the three countries have built an open platform for cooperation and adopted measures to facilitate trade, which has ensured steady growth. China has now become the largest trading partner of both Russia and Mongolia.

The priority of the CMREC is subregional cooperation in their adjacent regions to leverage comparative strengths, further boost multilateral investment and trade, promote exchanges in education, science and technology, and tourism, steadily advance the construction of overseas cooperative zones, and thus provide successful examples for regional economic cooperation.

新亚欧大陆桥经济走廊

新亚欧大陆桥，又名“第二亚欧大陆桥”，是横跨亚欧两大洲、连接太平洋和大西洋的国际大通道。新亚欧大陆桥经济走廊东起江苏连云港、山东日照等中国沿海港口城市，西至荷兰鹿特丹、比利时安特卫普等欧洲口岸，途经哈萨克斯坦、俄罗斯、白俄罗斯、波兰、德国等国家和地区，全长约10900千米，辐射亚欧大陆30多个国家和地区。

20世纪90年代初，新亚欧大陆桥初步开通。“一带一路”有力推动了新亚欧大陆桥建设，为沿线国家和亚欧两大洲经济贸易交流提供了便捷的大通道。新亚欧大陆桥经济走廊建设以中欧班列等现代化国际物流体系为依托，重点发展经贸和产能合作，拓展能源资源合作空间，构建畅通高效的区域大市场。

作为“一带一路”建设的标志性项目，渝新欧、蓉新欧、义新欧等多条中欧班列已经开通。其中，渝新欧从重庆出发，通过波兰抵达德国杜伊斯堡；蓉新欧从成都出发，抵达波兰；义新欧则从浙江义乌出发，抵达西班牙首都马德里。新亚欧大陆桥建设还同步推进相关公路交通、输电线

New Eurasian Land Bridge Economic Corridor

The New Eurasian Land Bridge (NELB) is an international passageway extending across the Eurasian continent and linking the Pacific and the Atlantic. It goes from China's coastal cities of Lianyungang and Rizhao to the Netherlands' Rotterdam and Belgium's Antwerp. The 10,900-kilometer-long rail link runs through Kazakhstan, Russia, Belarus, Poland and Germany, and serves more than 30 countries and regions.

Opened in the early 1990s, the NELB is gaining new impetus from the BRI. It greatly facilitates trade and economic exchanges among the countries along the route and between Asia and Europe. The NELB economic corridor relies on the China Railway Express to Europe and other modern international logistics systems to increase trade and industrial cooperation, expand energy resource cooperation, and build a regional market based on smooth, efficient transport.

To date, freight trains under the unified brand of "China Railway Express to Europe," as hallmark projects of the BRI, have entered service. These include the Chongqing-Xinjiang-Europe Express (reaching Germany's Duisburg via Poland), the Chengdu-Xinjiang-Europe Express (reaching Poland), and the Yiwu-Xinjiang-Europe Express (reaching Spain's Madrid). The construction of associated highways,

路、港口建设等方面的建设和运营。近年来，中国已经与新亚欧大陆桥经济走廊沿线多个国家签订了共建“一带一路”合作文件，有力促进亚欧两大洲经济贸易交流。

power transmission lines, and ports is progressing, with some already coming into operation. China has signed BRI cooperation agreements with a number of countries located along the NELB economic corridor, and this will strengthen Eurasian economic and trade exchanges.

中国—中亚—西亚经济走廊

中国—中亚—西亚经济走廊东起中国，向西至阿拉伯半岛，是中国与中亚和西亚各国之间形成的一个经济合作区域，大致与古丝绸之路范围相吻合。中国—中亚—西亚经济走廊从新疆出发，穿越中亚地区，抵达波斯湾、地中海沿岸和阿拉伯半岛，主要涉及中亚五国（哈萨克斯坦、吉尔吉斯斯坦、塔吉克斯坦、乌兹别克斯坦、土库曼斯坦）、伊朗、土耳其等国，是丝绸之路经济带的重要组成部分。通过中国—中亚—西亚经济走廊建设，打通该地区对外经贸合作和资金流动通道，有利于促进相关国家经济社会发展。

近年来，中国—中亚—西亚经济走廊上的重点项目得到实质性推进，区域合作取得了显著成效。在能源合作方面，中亚天然气管道中的三条线路管道已通气投产，预计第四条管道修建完成后，每年可从中亚国家输送到中国的天然气占中国同期消费总量的20%以上。此外，中国企业已向塔吉克斯坦交付10余项电力工程，基本解决了当地持续20年的电力紧张问题，实现四季供电可靠、冬季不再寒冷。在基础

China-Central Asia-West Asia Economic Corridor

The China-Central Asia-West Asia Economic Corridor (CCWAEC) links China and the Arabian Peninsula. The vast region it covers generally follows the trajectory of the ancient Silk Road.

The corridor starts from China's Xinjiang and traverses Central Asia before reaching the Persian Gulf, the Mediterranean Sea, and the Arabian Peninsula. It crosses five Central Asian countries (Kazakhstan, Kyrgyzstan, Tajikistan, Uzbekistan and Turkmenistan) and other countries (including Iran and Türkiye). It is an important component of the Silk Road Economic Belt. The CCWAEC will facilitate economic and trade cooperation and flow of capital to these regions and boost local economic and social development.

Substantial progress has been made on the key CCWAEC projects. In terms of energy cooperation, three natural gas pipelines extending across Central Asia have been completed and come into service. After the fourth pipeline is completed, natural gas transported from Central Asia to China will account for more than 20 percent of China's annual consumption. Chinese enterprises have delivered around a dozen power projects to Tajikistan, which have eased the power shortage that had remained a local headache for 20 years. There is stable power supply

设施建设方面，中国企业承建的乌兹别克斯坦卡姆奇克隧道是中亚迄今最长的一条铁路隧道，用中国技术、中国标准克服地质环境复杂、施工任务艰险等困难，成为共建“一带一路”互联互通合作示范性项目。新疆霍尔果斯国际邮件交换站于2022年7月正式运营，国际邮件进出境在此实现直接集散分拨，运递时效大幅提升。在国际运输方面，已开通的近30条中亚班列，为中国、中亚贸易往来和区域产品出口全球提供便利。

throughout the year, and heating has become available to local households in winter.

In terms of infrastructure, as a Chinese company has contracted the Qamchiq Tunnel, the longest railway tunnel in Central Asia, Chinese technology and standards have been applied to overcome the complex geological difficulties in Uzbekistan. This has become a signature BRI connectivity project.

Another example is the opening of China's Horgos international mail exchange station in July 2022, which has greatly increased delivery efficiency. In transcontinental transport, almost 30 freight trains now run between China and Central Asia, facilitating trade between the two sides and export of local products to other places around the world.

中国—中南半岛经济走廊

中南半岛与中国陆海相连，有几千年的历史渊源，有很强的地缘、人缘和文缘关系，是联通“一带一路”的重要桥梁和纽带。中国—中南半岛经济走廊以广西南宁和云南昆明为起点，以新加坡为终点，纵贯中南半岛的越南、老挝、柬埔寨、泰国、缅甸、马来西亚等国家，是中国连接中南半岛的大陆桥，也是中国与东盟合作的跨国经济走廊。中国—中南半岛经济走廊以沿线中心城市为依托，以铁路、公路为载体和纽带，以人员、物资、资金、信息的流通为基础，开拓新的战略通道和空间，加快形成优势互补、区域分工、共同发展的区域经济体。

2016年5月,《中国—中南半岛经济走廊倡议书》在第九届泛北部湾经济合作论坛上发布。携手共建中国—中南半岛经济走廊有利于打造新的区域增长点，促进中南半岛沿线国家的共同繁荣发展，也有利于构建中国—东盟命运共同体。

近年来，随着中国西部陆海新通道、中缅印度洋海公

China-Indochina Peninsula Economic Corridor

China and the Indochina Peninsula are connected by land and sea, with close geographical, cultural and people-to-people ties. The Indochina Peninsula is an important link on the Belt and Road.

The China-Indochina Peninsula Economic Corridor (CICPEC) extends from China's Nanning and Kunming to Singapore. This land bridge links China with the Indochina Peninsula and crosses the heart of Vietnam, Laos, Cambodia, Thailand, Myanmar and Malaysia. It is expected to boost China's cooperation with the ASEAN countries.

The CICPEC projects aim to connect cities in this region through a network of railways and highways to facilitate the flow of people, goods, capital, and information. It will open up new opportunities for strategic cooperation and create a regional economy bolstered by complementary strengths to ensure sound regional development.

In May 2016, the Proposal on the Joint Building of the China-Indochina Peninsula Economic Corridor was released at the Ninth Pan-Beibu Gulf Economic Cooperation Forum. By creating new regional growth drivers, it will help achieve common prosperity on the peninsula and strengthen the China-ASEAN community of shared future.

In recent years, with the construction of the New International Land-Sea Trade Corridor in western China, the

铁联运物流大通道、中老铁路的建设，中国—中南半岛经济走廊正成为联通中国与世界的又一纽带。依托中国—中南半岛经济走廊和中国西部陆海新通道建设，中国西部地区和新加坡等东盟国家间经北部湾港串联起的铁海联运主干线，由2017年的1条扩容至13条，并实现了主要港区进港铁路全覆盖。中缅印度洋海公铁联运物流大通道于2021年8月试运行成功，中老铁路于2021年12月开通，这些国际物流通道的打通，不仅为中国和东盟提供了便捷的贸易通道，还辐射到世界其他地区，带动了区域经济发展。

sea-highway-railway logistics transport system that links China, Myanmar and the Indian Ocean, and the China-Laos Railway, the CICPEC has become another belt connecting China and the rest of the world. Relying on the CICPEC and China's New International Land-Sea Trade Corridor, the railway-sea transport trunk lines linking western China and Singapore and other ASEAN countries via the Beibu Gulf have increased from one in 2017 to the current 13, with railways now reaching all the main ports. The sea-highway-railway logistics transport system linking China, Myanmar and the Indian Ocean began pilot operations in August 2021, and the China-Laos Railway came into service in December 2021. These have provided convenient trade channels for China and ASEAN and the rest of the world, and boosted regional economic development.

中巴经济走廊

中巴经济走廊是“一带一路”的旗舰项目。走廊起点位于中国新疆喀什，终点在巴基斯坦瓜达尔港，北接丝绸之路经济带，南连21世纪海上丝绸之路，是贯通南北丝路的关键枢纽，也是一条包括公路、铁路、油气管道和光缆覆盖的“四位一体”通道和贸易走廊。中巴经济走廊有助于促进整个南亚的互联互通，可使南亚、中亚、北非、海湾国家等通过经济、能源领域的合作紧密联合起来。

2015年4月，习近平和时任巴基斯坦总理纳瓦兹·谢里夫举行了中巴经济走廊五大项目动工仪式，并签订了近40项涉及中巴经济走廊的合作协议和备忘录。2017年12月，中巴两国共同编制的《中巴经济走廊远景规划》在伊斯兰堡发布。

近年来，中巴经济走廊成果主要集中在交通基础设施、能源、产业发展、农业、社会民生等领域。例如，瓜达尔东湾快速路建成通车，中国援瓜达尔海水淡化厂顺利开工；拉

China-Pakistan Economic Corridor

The China-Pakistan Economic Corridor (CPEC) is a flagship project under the BRI.

The corridor starts from China's Kashi and ends at Pakistan's Gwadar Port, and connects the Silk Road Economic Belt in the north and the 21st Century Maritime Silk Road in the south. It is a corridor of trade facilitated by a network of highways, railways, pipelines, and optical cables. While improving connectivity in South Asia, the corridor also helps link economic and energy cooperation between countries in South and Central Asia, North Africa, and along the Persian Gulf.

China's President Xi Jinping and Pakistan's Prime Minister Nawaz Sharif were present at the ground-breaking ceremony for five major projects in April 2015, when almost 40 agreements and memoranda relating to CPEC cooperation were signed. A jointly drafted long-term plan on the construction of the corridor was unveiled in December 2017.

In recent years, CPEC projects have concentrated on transport infrastructure, energy, industry, agriculture, and people's wellbeing. For instance, the Gwadar Eastbay Expressway has been completed and opened to traffic, the China-aided Gwadar Seawater Desalination Plant has started construction, the Lahore Orange Line Metro and

合尔橙线、白沙瓦—卡拉奇高速公路（苏库尔—木尔坦段）运行良好；卡洛特水电站全面投入商业运营，走廊项下已商业运行的12个能源合作项目为巴基斯坦提供了近三分之一的电力供应。截至2022年，中国连续7年成为巴基斯坦最大贸易伙伴，连续8年成为巴基斯坦最大投资来源国，中巴经济走廊累计为巴基斯坦带来254亿美元直接投资，创造了19.2万个就业岗位。在抗击新冠肺炎疫情期间，中国和巴基斯坦患难与共、真诚互助，两国“铁杆”情谊得到进一步升华。

the Peshawar-Karachi Motorway (Sukkur-Multan section) are running very well, and the Karot Hydropower Plant has come into full commercial operation. The 12 CPEC energy projects now provide almost one-third of Pakistan's power supply.

By 2022, China had been Pakistan's largest trading partner for seven years and the largest investor for eight consecutive years. The CPEC had attracted US$25.4 billion worth of direct investment for Pakistan and created 192,000 jobs. In their fight against Covid-19, China and Pakistan helped each other, and their friendship was further cemented.

孟中印缅经济走廊

2013年5月，中国、印度两国共同倡议建设孟中印缅经济走廊，推动中印两个大市场更紧密连接，加强该地区互联互通。这一倡议得到孟加拉国、缅甸两国的积极响应。同年12月，孟中印缅经济走廊联合研究工作组第一次会议在中国昆明召开，各方签署了孟中印缅经济走廊联合研究计划，正式建立了四国政府推进孟中印缅合作的机制。2014年9月，习近平在访问印度期间同莫迪总理会谈时提出中印双方要加快推进孟中印缅经济走廊建设，开展在“一带一路”框架内的合作。孟中印缅经济走廊不仅直接惠及四国，其辐射作用有助于带动南亚、东南亚、东亚三大经济板块联合发展。

近年来，孟中印缅经济走廊取得丰硕成果，对促进区域互联互通和多边合作发挥积极作用。中缅油气管道、莱比塘铜矿、达贡山镍矿等重大项目建成投产，为中缅互利共赢

Bangladesh-China-India-Myanmar Economic Corridor

The proposal for the Bangladesh-China-India-Myanmar Economic Corridor (BCIMEC) was unveiled by China and India in May 2013, with the objective of linking these two huge markets and improving regional connectivity. Bangladesh and Myanmar also welcomed the proposal.

In December 2013, the BCIMEC joint study group held its first meeting in Kunming, China, and a joint study plan was signed by all parties, leading to the establishment of a mechanism for cooperation among the four governments.

When meeting with Prime Minister Narendra Modi in India in September 2014, Xi Jinping suggested that China and India spearhead a joint effort to accelerate the construction of the BCIMEC under the framework of the BRI.

In addition to direct benefits to the four countries, the BCIMEC is expected to boost the integrated development of the three economic plates of South, Southeast, and East Asia.

In recent years, the BCIMEC has come to full fruition and greatly improved regional connectivity and multilateral cooperation. The China-Myanmar oil and gas pipelines, the Letpadaung copper mine, the Tagaung Taung nickel mine and other major projects have been completed and

树立了典范。中缅印度洋新通道海公铁联运于2021年8月首发，打通了连接环印度洋—缅甸仰光港—中国清水河口岸—临沧火车站—国内各地的贸易物流新通道，并相继开通运行多条海公铁联运/公铁联运国际线路。象征中孟友谊的标志性项目帕德玛大桥于2022年6月建成通车，每年可为孟加拉国国内生产总值增长贡献1.23个百分点，被当地人民称为“梦想之桥”。

在经贸关系方面，中印、中孟、中缅贸易规模均实现了大幅增长，折射出地区合作的旺盛需求和巨大潜力。从2013年到2022年，中印贸易额从654.7亿美元增长到1359.8亿美元，中孟贸易额从103.1亿美元增长到277.9亿美元，中缅贸易额从101.5亿美元增长到251.5亿美元。

put into operation, setting examples for bilateral win-win cooperation. In August 2021, the sea-highway-railway transport system linking China, Myanmar and the Indian Ocean launched trial operations, which enabled goods to travel from the Indian Ocean to inland China via Yangon, a major port of Myanmar. It was followed by more international freight transport services beginning operation on relevant lines. In June 2022, the Padma Bridge, a symbolic project of China-Bangladesh friendship and hailed by the locals as a bridge of dreams, opened to traffic; it is expected to contribute 1.23 percentage points to Bangladesh's annual GDP growth.

The volumes of trade between China and India, Bangladesh and Myanmar have all seen large growth, revealing the great demand and huge potential of regional cooperation. From 2013 to 2022, the trade between China and India grew from US$65.47 billion to US$135.98 billion, that between China and Bangladesh from US$10.31 billion to US$27.79 billion, and that between China and Myanmar from US$10.15 billion to US$25.15 billion.

合作机制

Cooperation Mechanisms

“一带一路”国际合作高峰论坛

“一带一路”国际合作高峰论坛是“一带一路”提出以来最高规格的论坛活动，主要包括开幕式、圆桌峰会和高级别会议三个部分。论坛致力于实现三个目标：一是全面总结“一带一路”建设的积极进展，展现重要早期收获成果，进一步凝聚合作共识，巩固良好的合作态势；二是共商下一阶段重要合作举措，进一步推动各方加强发展战略对接，深化伙伴关系，实现联动发展；三是在推进中国经济社会发展和结构调整的同时，推动国际合作，实现合作共赢。

第一届“一带一路”国际合作高峰论坛于2017年5月在北京举行，主题为“加强国际合作，共建‘一带一路’，实现共赢发展”。论坛作为2017年中国重要的主场外交活动，对推动地区和国际合作具有显著意义。习近平出席论坛开幕式并发表题为《携手推进“一带一路”建设》的主旨演讲。来自140多个国家和80多个国际组织约1600名代表出席论坛。经梳理汇总，第一届高峰论坛成果清单主要涵盖政策沟

Belt and Road Forum for International Cooperation

This is the highest-level international event organized under the framework of the BRI. The main activities include an opening ceremony, a leaders' roundtable, and a high-level conference.

The event is designed for three purposes: first, to summarize progress in Belt and Road cooperation, present initial outcomes, build consensus, and maintain positive momentum in cooperation; second, to discuss major measures for further cooperation, further align the development strategies of individual parties, and expand partnerships for joint development; third, to promote international cooperation for win-win results along with China's economic and social development and structural adjustment.

China hosted the first forum in Beijing in May 2017. The theme was "Strengthening International Cooperation in Building the Belt and Road for Win-win Development." A major diplomatic gathering in 2017, it was significant to international and regional cooperation. At its opening ceremony, Xi Jinping delivered a keynote speech, "Work Together to Build the Silk Road Economic Belt and the 21st Century Maritime Silk Road." About 1,600 representatives from more than 140 countries and over 80 international organizations came to the event. The major deliverables

通、设施联通、贸易畅通、资金融通、民心相通5大类，共76大项270多项具体成果。

第二届“一带一路”国际合作高峰论坛于2019年4月在北京举行，主题为“共建‘一带一路’、开创美好未来”。来自150多个国家和90多个国际组织的6000余名外宾应约参会。第二届论坛的分论坛数量扩大到12场，比首届增加了一倍。除了首届原有的“五通”和“智库交流”六个主题外，新增廉洁、数字、绿色、创新、境外经贸合作区以及地方合作等主题，并首次举办“一带一路”企业家大会，印证着共建“一带一路”不断走深走实、行稳致远。习近平出席高峰论坛开幕式并发表主旨演讲，全程主持领导人圆桌峰会，同与会各国领导人举行了双边会见，宣示推动共建“一带一路”高质量发展的理念。作为中国2019年最重要的主场外交活动，第二届高峰论坛达成6大类283项务实成果，成为推动“一带一路”建设从“大写意”迈向“工笔画”的里程碑，为全球经济增长开辟更多空间，为构建人类命运共同体作出新贡献。与会各方普遍认为，“一带一路”国际合作高峰论坛是重要多边合作平台，支持高峰论坛常态化举办。

numbered over 270 in 76 categories regarding policy coordination, infrastructure connectivity, unimpeded trade, financial integration, and people-to-people ties.

The second forum was held in Beijing in April 2019. Its theme was “Belt and Road Cooperation: Shaping a Brighter Shared Future.” It attracted more than 6,000 people from over 150 countries and 90 international organizations. They attended 12 sessions, double the number of the first forum. The subjects of discussion included the five-pronged approach, think tank exchanges, clean Silk Road, digital Silk Road, green Silk Road, Silk Road of innovation, overseas economic and trade cooperation zones, and sub-national cooperation. A Belt and Road CEO conference was also organized. Xi Jinping delivered a keynote speech at the opening ceremony and presided over the Leaders' Roundtable. He also met the leaders of different countries and expounded on high-quality Belt and Road cooperation.

A significant diplomatic event for China in 2019, the forum concluded with 283 deliverables in six categories representing a milestone in the evolution of the BRI from a master plan to specific projects. These have opened wider space for global economic growth and for building a global community of shared future. The participants hailed the forum as a major platform for multilateral cooperation and supported its regular convention in the future.

上海合作组织

上海合作组织成立于2001年6月，创始成员国为中国、俄罗斯、哈萨克斯坦、吉尔吉斯斯坦、塔吉克斯坦、乌兹别克斯坦，现有9个成员国、3个观察员国、14个对话伙伴，是世界上幅员最广、人口最多的综合性区域合作组织，也是欧亚地区和国际事务中重要的建设性力量。

上海合作组织创造性地提出并始终遵循“上海精神”，主张互信、互利、平等、协商、尊重多样文明、谋求共同发展，致力于世界和平与发展和人类进步事业，为构建新型国际关系和人类命运共同体作出重要理论和实践探索。

作为“一带一路”倡议的积极支持者和践行者，上海合作组织坚持区域经济融合发展，推动共建“一带一路”倡议同各国发展战略及区域合作倡议对接，深入开展经贸、交通、农业、能源等领域合作，为各国经济发展和民生改善注入了不竭动力。

Shanghai Cooperation Organization

The Shanghai Cooperation Organization (SCO) was founded in Shanghai in June 2001, with six founding states – China, Russia, Kazakhstan, Kyrgyzstan, Tajikistan and Uzbekistan. It now has nine member states, three observer states and 14 dialogue partners, and has become a comprehensive organization for regional cooperation, covering a large population on vast territories and an important constructive force in Eurasian and international affairs.

The SCO members have developed the "Shanghai Spirit," which is based on mutual trust, mutual benefit, equality, consultation, respect for cultural diversity, and pursuit of common development. They are devoted to world peace and development and human progress, and have worked constructively on a new type of international relations and a global community of shared future.

As an active supporter of the BRI, the SCO has worked for regional economic integration, promoted the synergy of the BRI with the development strategies of individual countries and the regional cooperation initiatives, and conducted cooperation in economy and trade, transport, agriculture and energy. Its efforts have resulted in notable improvements in economic development and wellbeing.

中国—东盟“10+1”机制

中国—东盟“10+1”机制是中国与东南亚国家联盟建立的合作机制，自1997年成立以来，双方合作不断扩大与深化，现已发展成一个密切的政治、经济合作组织，成为东亚区域合作的主要机制之一。

1991年，中国与东盟开启对话进程。1997年，双方举行第一次“10+1”领导人会议，宣布建立中国—东盟睦邻互信伙伴关系。2010年1月，中国—东盟自贸区正式建成，这是双方关系史上的重大事件，开启了中国与东盟实现经济一体化的进程。自此，中国成为第一个加入《东南亚友好合作条约》和第一个同东盟建立战略伙伴关系的域外大国，也是第一个同东盟建成自贸区的大国。2021年11月，习近平和东盟国家领导人共同出席中国—东盟建立对话关系30周年纪念峰会，宣布建立中国东盟全面战略伙伴关系。

为保障双方合作的顺利与成效，中国—东盟“10+1”机制确立了一套完整的对话与合作平台，主要包括政府首脑

China-ASEAN (10+1) Cooperation Mechanism

Established in 1997, the China-ASEAN (10+1) Cooperation Mechanism has played an important role in promoting closer political and economic ties between China and ASEAN members, and has become one of the major mechanisms for regional cooperation.

China-ASEAN dialogue relations started in 1991. The first China-ASEAN (10+1) summit held in 1997 announced the formation of the China-ASEAN partnership of good-neighborliness and mutual trust. The China-ASEAN Free Trade Area was established in January 2010, representing a milestone in China-ASEAN bilateral relations and initiating the process of China-ASEAN economic integration. China was the first non-ASEAN country to join the Treaty of Amity and Cooperation in Southeast Asia and establish a strategic partnership with ASEAN, and the first major country to build a free trade area with ASEAN. In November 2021, Xi Jinping and the ASEAN state leaders attended the ASEAN-China Special Summit to Commemorate the 30th Anniversary of ASEAN-China Dialogue Relations and announced the establishment of a comprehensive strategic partnership between ASEAN and China.

Necessary platforms for dialogue have been created to ensure successful and effective bilateral cooperation,

会议、部长级会议、高官会等。中国—东盟中心是推进双方合作的重要常设机构。

东盟国家处于“一带一路”的陆海交汇地带，是中国推进“一带一路”建设的优先方向和重要伙伴。10年来，共建“一带一路”倡议在东盟国家落地生根、开花结果，中国和东盟国家不断加强战略对接，在经贸投资、互联互通、产能合作、绿色转型、数字经济等领域合作捷报频传，硕果累累，携手打造了高质量共建“一带一路”的东南亚样板。中国与东盟十国均已签署双边共建“一带一路”合作文件。《东盟互联互通总体规划2025》设定的可持续基础设施、数字创新、无缝衔接的物流、良好的规章制度、人员往来五大战略目标与“一带一路”倡议提出的政策沟通、设施联通、贸易畅通、资金融通、人心相通的“五通”理念高度契合。

including the ASEAN-China Summit, ministerial meetings, and senior officials' meetings. The ASEAN-China Center is a permanent body for promoting bilateral cooperation.

The ASEAN countries are located in the area where the Silk Road routes on the land meet those on the sea. They are a priority orientation and important partners of China in promoting Belt and Road cooperation. Since it was first proposed in 2013, the BRI has taken root and borne fruit in the ASEAN countries. China and ASEAN have strengthened synergy between their development strategies, and made substantial progress in trade and economic investment, connectivity, cooperation on industrial capacity, green transformation, and the digital economy. They have together created a successful example of Belt and Road cooperation in Southeast Asia. To date China has signed bilateral documents on Belt and Road cooperation with all of the 10 ASEAN countries. The Master Plan on ASEAN Connectivity 2025 and the China-proposed five-pronged approach under the BRI are highly consistent, particularly in terms of infrastructure, digital innovation, seamless dovetailing of logistics, sound regulations and rules, and people-to-people exchanges.

亚太经济合作组织

亚太经济合作组织（简称“亚太经合组织”）是亚太地区层级最高、领域最广、最具影响力的经济合作机制。1989年11月，澳大利亚、美国、日本、韩国、新西兰、加拿大及当时的东盟六国在澳大利亚首都堪培拉举行亚太经合组织首届部长级会议，标志着亚太经合组织正式成立。1991年11月，中国正式加入亚太经合组织。亚太经合组织现有21个成员和3个观察员。

作为经济论坛，亚太经合组织主要讨论与全球和区域经济有关的议题，其宗旨是支持亚太区域经济可持续增长和繁荣，建设活力和谐的亚太大家庭，捍卫自由开放的贸易和投资，加速区域经济一体化进程，鼓励经济技术合作，保障人民安全，促进建设良好和可持续的商业环境。亚太经合组织共有5个层次的运作机制：领导人非正式会议、部长级会议、高官会、委员会和工作组、秘书处。

作为“一带一路”建设的多边依托机制，亚太经合组织与“一带一路”倡议在很多领域目标一致。亚太经合组织推进亚太互联互通建设已成为“一带一路”框架下设施联通

Asia-Pacific Economic Cooperation

The Asia-Pacific Economic Cooperation (APEC) is the premier and most extensive and influential mechanism for economic cooperation in the Asia-Pacific region.

The inaugural forum was held in November 1989 at a ministerial meeting in the Australian capital of Canberra, attended by Australia, the US, Japan, the Republic of Korea, New Zealand, Canada, and the then six ASEAN countries. China became an APEC member in November 1991. APEC now has 21 member economies and three observers.

As an economic forum, APEC focuses on global and regional economic issues. Its mission is to support sustainable economic growth and prosperity in the Asia-Pacific region and build a dynamic and harmonious Asia-Pacific community by championing free and open trade and investment, accelerating regional economic integration, encouraging economic and technical cooperation, ensuring human security, and facilitating a favorable and sustainable business environment. APEC operates at five institutional levels: meetings of economic leaders, ministerial meetings, senior officials' meetings, committees and working groups, and the Secretariat.

The goals of APEC, as a multilateral mechanism for cooperation, are very much in line with the BRI. APEC projects to improve Asia-Pacific connectivity are also an

的重要组成部分。亚太经合组织推进亚太地区包容性增长与“一带一路”框架下推动沿线国家经济可持续发展相辅相成。

important part of the BRI projects to improve infrastructure connectivity, and APEC efforts to advance inclusive Asia-Pacific growth are complementary to the sustainable economic development of the BRI participating countries.

亚洲合作对话

亚洲合作对话是目前唯一面向全亚洲的官方对话与合作机制，成立于2002年，旨在推动各成员之间农业、能源、扶贫等领域的交流与合作，通过开展亚洲对话推动亚洲合作、促进亚洲发展。亚洲合作对话机制现有35个成员国。亚洲合作对话机制以领导人会议、外长会议、领域牵头国、高级研究小组会等形式开展活动，目前已召开了两次领导人会议和17次外长会议。

亚洲合作对话成员国都是陆上丝绸之路和海上丝绸之路沿线国家，合作理念、方向、领域与“一带一路”高度契合，是推动共建“一带一路”的合作伙伴。高质量共建“一带一路”也将丰富亚洲合作对话的内涵。

Asia Cooperation Dialogue

The Asia Cooperation Dialogue (ACD) is the only mechanism for official dialogue and cooperation covering the whole of Asia. Inaugurated in 2002, it aims to promote exchanges in areas such as agriculture, energy, and poverty reduction and boost Asia-wide cooperation and development through dialogue.

The ACD has 35 member states. Its activities are conducted through the summits, foreign ministers' meetings, prime movers in specific areas, and meetings of high-level study groups. Two ACD Summits and 17 Foreign Ministers' Meetings have been held.

ACD states are all located along the Belt and Road routes, and their vision, orientation, and fields of cooperation are highly consistent with those under the BRI. This makes them natural partners in promoting the BRI, and high-quality Belt and Road cooperation will also enrich ACD activities in return.

中阿合作论坛与中阿峰会

2004年1月，中国和阿拉伯国家联盟共同宣布成立“中国—阿拉伯国家合作论坛”（简称“中阿合作论坛”），旨在加强对话与合作、促进和平与发展。中阿合作论坛成员国包括中国和阿盟22个成员国，组织机构包括部长级会议、高官会、联络组等。

2014年6月，习近平在中阿合作论坛第六届部长级会议开幕式上指出，成立中阿合作论坛是着眼中阿关系长远发展作出的战略抉择，论坛已成为丰富中阿关系战略内涵、推进中阿务实合作的有效抓手。2016年5月，中阿合作论坛第七届部长级会议在卡塔尔多哈举行。习近平和卡塔尔埃米尔塔米姆分别致贺信。会议围绕“共建‘一带一路’，深化中阿战略合作”议题，就中阿关系发展和中阿合作论坛建设达成广泛共识。2018年7月，习近平在中阿合作论坛第八届部长级会议上宣布中阿双方建立全面合作、共同发展、面向未来的中阿战略伙伴关系。会议通过并签署《中阿合作共建“一

China-Arab States Cooperation Forum and China-Arab States Summit

China and the League of Arab States jointly announced in January 2004 the launch of the China-Arab States Cooperation Forum (CASCF) for the purpose of increasing dialogue and cooperation and promoting peace and development. CASCF members include China and the 22 member states of the Arab League, and its organizational structure is composed of ministerial conferences, senior officials' meetings and liaison groups.

Addressing the opening of the Sixth CASCF Ministerial Conference in June 2014, Xi Jinping characterized the CASCF as of strategic importance for the long-term development of bilateral relations and substantive cooperation.

In May 2016, during the Seventh CASCF Ministerial Conference in Doha, capital of Qatar, President Xi Jinping and Qatari Emir Sheikh Tamim each sent a letter of congratulations. Under the theme of "Jointly Building the Belt and Road to Reinforce Strategic Cooperation," the meeting reached a broad consensus on bilateral relations and the future work of the CASCF.

At the Eighth CASCF Ministerial Conference held in July 2018, Xi Jinping declared that the two sides had agreed to establish a future-oriented Sino-Arab strategic partnership of comprehensive cooperation and common development. The meeting adopted and signed the Declaration of Action

带一路”行动宣言》等重要成果文件。

在中阿合作论坛的基础上，2022年12月，首届中国一阿拉伯国家峰会（简称“中阿峰会”）在沙特利雅得举行。习近平和20多位阿盟成员国领导人、国际组织负责人出席峰会，明确将全力构建面向新时代的中阿命运共同体作为中国和阿拉伯国家的共同意愿、目标、行动。会议发表的《首届中阿峰会利雅得宣言》提出，共同落实“一带一路”倡议，为双方合作和发展提供广阔机遇，努力推动“一带一路”倡议与各阿拉伯国家发展愿景对接，实现互利共赢。

中国与阿拉伯国家发展阶段衔接、理念思路契合、经济结构互补，中国多年稳居阿拉伯国家第一大贸易伙伴国地位。共建“一带一路”顺应阿拉伯国家推进经济多元化和工业化的发展需求。目前，中国已同21个阿拉伯国家以及阿盟签署共建“一带一路”合作文件，在能源、基础设施等领域实施200多个大型合作项目，合作成果惠及双方近20亿人民。

on China-Arab States Cooperation under the Belt and Road Initiative.

Under the auspices of the CASCF, the First China-Arab States Summit was held in the Saudi capital Riyadh. Leaders of China and the member states of the League and heads of some international organizations attended. They made it clear that building a China-Arab community of shared future in the new era is the shared wish, goal, and action for China and the Arab states. In a declaration issued at the summit, they said they would continue to implement BRI projects, create opportunities for bilateral cooperation and common development, and harmonize the BRI and their development visions for win-win results.

China and the Arab states are complementary to each other in terms of development stage, development philosophy, and economic structure, and China has become the largest trading partner of some of the Arab states. As the BRI projects respond to economic diversification and industrialization in the Arab states, China has signed Belt and Road cooperation documents with the Arab League and 21 of its members. Over 200 large Belt and Road projects have been carried out in energy and infrastructure, benefiting nearly 2 billion people on the two sides.

中非合作论坛

在中非双方共同倡议下，2000年10月，中非合作论坛第一届部长级会议在北京召开，中非合作论坛正式成立。论坛以平等磋商、增进了解、扩大共识、加强友谊、促进合作为宗旨，成员包括中国、与中国建交的53个非洲国家以及非洲联盟委员会，会议机制包括部长级会议、高官会等。

中非合作论坛是中国和非洲国家开展集体对话、深化互利合作的重要渠道，也是世界上规模最大、成效最好的南南合作平台。中非双方共建“一带一路”，为中非互利合作注入新的强劲动力，把中非互利合作提升至新的水平，将中非全面战略合作伙伴关系推进至新的阶段。2021年11月中非合作论坛第八届部长级会议以来，中非双方继续推进基础设施建设合作。合作项目包括已投入运营的喀麦隆克里比-罗拉贝高速公路和尼日利亚莱基深水港项目，以及一、二期通车的埃及“斋月十日城”市郊铁路等。

Forum on China-Africa Cooperation

The Forum on China-Africa Cooperation (FOCAC) is a joint initiative between China and Africa. It was inaugurated at its first ministerial conference in October 2000 in Beijing. It promotes understanding, consensus, friendship and cooperation through equal consultation. Its members include China, the 53 African states that have established diplomatic relations with China, and the Commission of the African Union. The FOCAC mechanism includes ministerial conferences and senior officials' meetings.

FOCAC is an important channel for the collective dialogue between China and the African countries to expand mutually beneficial cooperation. It is the world's largest and most effective platform for South-South cooperation. China-Africa collaboration under the BRI has added strong impetus to mutually beneficial cooperation and upgraded their comprehensive strategic and cooperative partnership.

Since the Eighth FOCAC Ministerial Conference held in November 2021, the two sides have continued to advance cooperation on infrastructure construction. The cooperative projects include the Kribi-Lolabe Highway in Cameroon, the Lekki Deep-sea Port in Nigeria, and the 10th of Ramadan City light rail transit in Egypt, which have all come into operation.

目前，中国已同52个非洲国家及非盟委员会签署共建“一带一路”合作文件。“一带一路”合作在对接非洲自身发展需要和规划的同时，不仅帮助非洲增强自身“造血”功能，也为相关国家产业升级和发展奠定了坚实基础，支持非洲实现可持续发展。

China has signed Belt and Road cooperation documents with 52 African states and the Commission of the African Union. Their cooperation meets Africa's development needs and harmonizes bilateral plans. It will help Africa increase its own development capacity and lay solid foundations for industrial upgrading and sustainable development for participating countries.

合作案例
Projects Under Way

中老铁路

中老铁路是中国“一带一路”倡议与老挝“变陆锁国为陆联国”战略对接的重要项目，也是以中方为主投资建设、全线采用中国技术标准、使用中国设备并与中国铁路网直接连通的国际铁路。中老铁路全长1035千米，线路北起昆明，过中国磨憨铁路口岸和老挝磨丁铁路口岸，进入老挝北部地区，最后到达老挝首都万象。

2021年12月，中老铁路全线开通运营，中老之间互联互通实现跨越式发展。2023年4月，中老铁路跨境客运列车开行，中国昆明—老挝万象实现乘火车当日通达。2023年7月，“澜湄蓉欧快线”班列载运货物搭乘中老铁路入境，经申报转关再转乘中欧班列出境，这标志着依托“中老铁路+

China-Laos Railway

The China-Laos Railway is a major project that docks China's BRI and Laos' strategy to transform itself from a landlocked country to a land-linked hub. With China as the main investor, it is an international line built with Chinese technical standards and equipment and directly linked to China's rail network. Starting from China's Kunming in the north and running southward across the Mohan and Boten crossings at the China-Laos border, the 1,035-kilometer line travels through northern Laos before reaching its capital Vientiane in the south.

The entire railway began operation in December 2021, marking a leap forward in China-Laos connectivity. In April 2023, it started cross-border passenger services, enabling people to travel between Kunming and Vientiane within one day on the bullet train.

In July 2023, a fully loaded Lancang-Mekong-Chengdu-Europe freight train entered China via the China-Laos Railway, and after simplified customs transit procedures were completed, the goods were transferred to a China-Europe freight train heading for Europe. This was the first batch of transit goods transported using the China-Laos Railway and the China-Europe Railway Express. It is just one example of the convenient trade and economic exchanges along the Belt and Road routes that have become possible thanks

中欧班列”打造的纵跨亚欧大陆国际物流运输体系正在加快建设，“一带一路”沿线经贸往来将更加通畅。

中老铁路深刻改变了老挝交通运输格局，对密切中老两国经济社会和人文合作交流，加快建设中老经济走廊、构建中老命运共同体，具有十分重要的意义。作为泛亚铁路的重要骨干，中老铁路还将对中国—东盟自由贸易区、大湄公河次区域经济合作产生积极影响。

to the construction of the Eurasian international logistics transport system.

The China-Laos Railway has greatly changed transport conditions in Laos. It is central to increasing bilateral economic, social, cultural and people-to-people exchanges and building the China-Laos economic corridor and community of shared future. As a trunk line in the trans-Asian railway network, it will contribute to the China-ASEAN Free Trade Area and the Greater Mekong Subregion Economic Cooperation.

中泰铁路

中泰铁路是中国与泰国合作建设的泰国首条标准轨高速铁路，采用中国标准设计建造，一期工程连接曼谷和呵叻，二期工程将延伸至东北边贸重镇廊开，并实现与中老铁路衔接。

2012年，时任泰国总理英拉访华，两国提出“大米换高铁”计划。2014年12月，泰国国家立法议会批准中泰铁路合作谅解备忘录草案。同年12月，中泰两国总理共同见证了《中泰铁路合作谅解备忘录》的签署，随后，中泰铁路进入正式协商阶段。2015年12月，中泰铁路项目在泰国举行了启动仪式。2017年12月，中泰铁路一期工程（曼谷—呵叻段）正式开工建设，全长约252.3千米，设计时速250千米。多年来，中泰铁路合作联合委员会围绕中泰铁路合作项目一期工作进展、二期（呵叻—廊开）合作模式，以及中老

China-Thailand Railway

The China-Thailand Railway will enable Thailand to have its first standard-gauge high-speed railway, which will be jointly built by China and Thailand. The first phase connects Bangkok and Nakhon Ratchasima, and the second phase will extend to Nong Khai, a trade town in northeast Thailand, and connect with the China-Laos Railway in the north.

A "rice for high-speed rail" plan was proposed by both countries in 2012 during Thai Prime Minister Yingluck Shinawatra's visit to China. After approval by the Thai parliament in December 2014, a memorandum of understanding for the rail project was signed in the presence of the Chinese premier and the Thai prime minister. This was followed by formal consultation on the project.

A ground-breaking ceremony was held in Thailand in December 2015. The construction of the 252-kilometer Bangkok-Nakhon Ratchasima section began in December 2017, with a designed speed of 250 kilometers per hour. In July 2022, the first extra-large bridge of the first phase was completed.

Over the past years, the China-Thailand joint committee on railway cooperation has conducted negotiations on the first phase progress and the model of cooperation for the second phase, and the extension to connect with the China-Laos

泰铁路连接线等问题进行了多轮深入磋商。2022年7月，中泰铁路一期工程首座特大桥完成架设。

中泰铁路是两国开展“一带一路”合作、开展产能合作的旗舰项目。中泰铁路建成后，一方面将促进地区互联互通建设，另一方面有利于沿线地区根据各自优势探讨建设边境经济特区、产业园区、物流中心等，从而使经济发展滞后的内陆地区能够搭乘地区经济快车，挖掘和释放经济潜力，对解决地区发展不均衡问题、促进整体繁荣意义重大。随着中泰铁路合作项目和双方各领域务实合作持续深入推进，中泰友好关系将迈上新台阶。

Railway.

This railway is a showcase for bilateral cooperation on industrial capacity under the BRI. It is expected to help improve regional connectivity, and enable the local regions to leverage their respective strengths and explore the possibility of building border special economic zones, industrial parks, and logistics centers. The project will address the development imbalance and promote common prosperity, as it will offer opportunities for backward inland regions to board the regional economic expressway and tap their potential.

Along with the progress of this project and bilateral cooperation in other fields, China-Thailand friendship will reach new heights.

蒙内铁路

蒙内铁路是东非铁路网的起始段，全长约480千米，设计客运时速120千米、货运时速80千米，连接肯尼亚首都内罗毕和东非第一大港蒙巴萨港，是肯尼亚独立以来最大的基础设施建设项目，也是“一带一路”倡议在非洲落地的重要成果。

蒙内铁路全线采用中国标准、中国技术、中国装备，是肯尼亚百年来修建的第一条新铁路，所以有该国“世纪铁路”之称。蒙内铁路于2014年10月正式开工建设，2017年5月正式通车。截至2023年8月，蒙内铁路累计发送旅客1100万人次，累计发送货物2800万吨。为了保护当地生态环境和野生动物，蒙内铁路在设计中严格遵循肯尼亚的相关整体规划，注重保持当地原有的自然风貌，将人与自然和谐共生的理念融于铁路建设和运营各环节，树立了共建“一带一路”的绿色标杆。

蒙内铁路是落实“一带一路”倡议和中非合作论坛约翰内斯堡峰会“十大合作计划”的重要早期收获，是中非“三

Mombasa-Nairobi Railway

The 480-kilometer-long Mombasa-Nairobi Railway is the first section of a planned East Africa railway network. Passenger trains travel at 120 kilometers per hour, while freight trains run at 80 kilometers per hour. Connecting Kenya's capital city of Nairobi with Mombasa, the largest port in East Africa, it is the largest infrastructure project in Kenya since its independence in 1963. It is also a major BRI project in Africa. Built with Chinese standards, technology and equipment, it is the first new rail line in Kenya in a century.

Construction started in October 2014, and the railway entered service in May 2017. By August 2023, it had transported 11 million passengers and 28 million tons of goods. To protect the local eco-environment and wild animals, the designers strictly followed Kenyan plans, gave consideration to the original natural landscape, and incorporated the idea of harmonious coexistence of humanity with nature into the construction and operation of the railway. This has made the project a benchmark for green Belt and Road cooperation.

The railway is an early outcome of the BRI and of the 10 cooperation plans devised at the FOCAC Johannesburg Summit in 2015. It is a hallmark of China-Africa cooperation in industrialization, industrial capacity, and building

网一化”和产能合作的标志性工程。建成后，蒙巴萨到内罗毕之间的旅程从原先的10多个小时缩短到4个多小时，物流成本降低40%以上。铁路的成功运营全面带动了肯尼亚经济社会发展，带动其GDP增长2%以上，推进了当地大型基础设施建设同产业发展的良性互促。

根据规划，蒙内铁路延伸线未来将连接肯尼亚、坦桑尼亚、乌干达、卢旺达、布隆迪、南苏丹和埃塞俄比亚等东非7国，成为连接非洲沿海与内陆的重要交通线，促进东非现代化铁路网建设和地区经济社会发展。

networks of high-speed railway, expressway, and regional civil aviation.

It has cut the travel time between Mombasa and Nairobi from over 10 hours to about four hours and reduced the cost of movement of goods by 40 percent. Its success has driven Kenya's economic and social development and boosted annual GDP growth by 2 percent, demonstrating the mutual reinforcement of large infrastructure and industrial development.

A long-term master plan envisions a rail system connecting seven East African countries: Kenya, Tanzania, Uganda, Rwanda, Burundi, South Sudan and Ethiopia. This will serve as an important link between coastal and inland Africa and promote the construction of a modern railway network and the economic and social development in East Africa.

匈塞铁路

匈塞铁路是共建“一带一路”倡议与欧洲发展战略对接的重大项目。匈塞铁路连接匈牙利首都布达佩斯和塞尔维亚首都贝尔格莱德，全长近350千米，原线路始建于19世纪末。经现代化改造之后，匈塞铁路将成为客货共用电气化双线铁路，设计最高时速200千米。建成通车后，贝尔格莱德和布达佩斯两地之间的旅程将从目前的8小时缩短至3小时以内，极大地提高该地区交通便利水平，助力区域经济发展。

2022年3月，匈塞铁路塞尔维亚境内贝诺段开通运营，线路全长约80千米，列车最高运行时速由原来的40至50千米提升至200千米，运输品质和效率极大提升，成为当地民众出行首选。

匈塞铁路是中国与中东欧国家共建“一带一路”的重点项目，实现中国铁路技术标准与欧盟铁路技术标准的良好对接。作为一条重要的国际线路，匈塞铁路有力推动中国—中东欧国家友好合作，促进区域互联互通、共同发展。

Hungary-Serbia Railway

The Hungary-Serbia Railway is a large project synergizing China's BRI and the European development strategy. Linking Hungarian capital Budapest and Serbian capital Belgrade, the 350-kilometer rail line was first built in the late 19th century. It will be renovated into an electrified passenger and freight railway, with the fastest designed speed of 200 kilometers per hour. This will shorten the travel time between the two cities from eight hours to less than three hours, greatly facilitate local transport, and boost regional economic growth.

The Serbian section of about 80 kilometers, between Belgrade and Novi Sad, entered service in March 2022. Trains are now traveling at 200 kilometers per hour, up from less than 50 kilometers per hour previously. This has greatly improved transport experience and efficiency and become a popular choice for the local residents.

The Hungary-Serbia Railway is a key BRI project undertaken by China and Central and Eastern European countries, which has applied the rail standards of both China and the European Union (EU). As a key international line, it will extend cooperation between China and Central and Eastern European countries and improve regional connectivity and shared development.

中国—白俄罗斯工业园

中国—白俄罗斯工业园（简称“中白工业园”）是目前中国参与投资开发的规划面积最大、开发建设规模最大的海外经贸合作区。2010年3月，习近平到访白俄罗斯，白俄罗斯政府希望能够借鉴中国—新加坡苏州工业园区的模式，在其境内建立中白工业园。2011年9月，两国政府签订了关于中白工业园的协定。2012年8月，中白工业园区开发股份有限公司成立。2014年6月，该工业园在明斯克奠基。

2015年5月，习近平在与白俄罗斯总统卢卡申科会谈时，建议推动两国发展战略对接，共建丝绸之路经济带，把中白工业园建设作为合作重点，发挥政府间协调机制作用，谋划好园区未来发展，将园区项目打造成丝绸之路经济带上的明珠和双方互利合作的典范。

中白工业园总面积达112.5平方千米，国际公路、洲际公路、铁路穿越园区，连接欧亚经济联盟与欧盟国家，具有

China-Belarus Industrial Park

The China-Belarus Industrial Park is the largest economic and trade cooperation zone financed overseas by China.

During Xi Jinping's visit to Belarus in March 2010, the Belarusian government expressed interest in opening an industrial park in Belarus modeled on the China-Singapore Industrial Park in Suzhou, Jiangsu Province. An agreement was signed by both governments in September 2011, and a joint venture, China-Belarus Industrial Park Development Company, was established in August 2012. A foundation stone laying ceremony was held in Minsk in June 2014.

During talks with Belarusian President Lukashenko in May 2015, Xi Jinping proposed expanding the strategic development alignment between China and Belarus in a joint effort to build the Silk Road Economic Belt, with the construction of the industrial park as a focal point. He emphasized the importance of coordination between both governments in planning the park to maximize the advantages of cooperation.

Occupying an area of 112.5 square kilometers, it is strategically situated, connecting the Eurasian Economic Union countries and the EU members and enjoying easy access to international and intercontinental highways and railways.

良好的区位优势。中白工业园以先进制造业和现代服务业为支撑，吸引和积聚智力资源，计划建成集“生态、宜居、兴业、活力、创新”五位一体的国际新城。截至2023年6月，中白工业园已有100余家企业入驻，协议投资总额超过13.3亿美元。

Focusing on advanced manufacturing and modern services and attracting international intellectual resources, the park is expected to become a new international city, an environmentally friendly, vibrant community that embraces entrepreneurship and innovation, and an ideal place to live in.

By June 2023, more than 100 enterprises had moved into the park, with their agreed investment surpassing US$1.33 billion.

瓜达尔港自由区

2016年11月，巴基斯坦瓜达尔港正式开航。作为“中巴经济走廊”重点项目之一和瓜达尔港开发项目的重要组成部分，瓜达尔港自由区以港口为依托，重点发展商贸物流、加工贸易、仓储和金融等产业。

瓜达尔港自由区总占地面积约为9.23平方千米，分四期进行建设。截至2022年6月，瓜达尔港自由区第一阶段已经建设完成，已有46家企业入驻，涵盖海外仓、化肥、渔业加工、金属材料制造、农业开发、旅游、保险、银行等领域，投资额超过30亿元人民币，可为当地提供近5000个就业机会。自由区第二阶段已于2021年7月启动，面积是第一阶段的36倍。

瓜达尔港自由区将采用类似深圳蛇口的建设模式，形成一个包括“港口+园区+城区”的综合体。建成后的瓜达尔港自由区将带动俾路支省乃至巴基斯坦全国的整体发展。

Gwadar Port Free Zone

The Gwadar Port in Pakistan came into service in November 2016. A key part of the China-Pakistan Economic Corridor and an essential component of the Gwadar Port development project, the adjacent free zone aims to improve trade logistics, facilitate processing trade, and promote warehousing and financial services.

The free zone, covering a planned area of 9.23 square kilometers, will be developed in four phases. By June 2022, the first phase had been completed, and 46 enterprises had moved in. Engaging in overseas warehousing, chemical fertilizers, fishery processing, metal materials, agricultural development, tourism, insurance, and banking, they represented a combined investment exceeding 3 billion yuan and had provided about 5,000 jobs for the local residents. The second phase began in July 2021, covering an area 36 times that of the first phase.

The free zone, comprising a port, an industrial park and residential and business areas, will be modeled on China's Shekou Industrial Zone. Once completed, it will spur economic growth in Balochistan and the rest of Pakistan.

科伦坡港口城

科伦坡港口城是中斯两国在“一带一路”建设中务实对接的重点项目，由中国企业和斯里兰卡政府联合开发，是斯里兰卡目前最大的外国投资项目。

科伦坡港口城毗邻斯里兰卡首都科伦坡中心商务区，占地面积2.69平方千米，通过在科伦坡港口附近填海造地的方式，规划金融区、中央公园区、宜居生活岛、游艇码头区、国际品牌带动区等五大主题区域；建造布局设计精湛的甲级写字楼、医疗中心、教育机构、休闲娱乐综合体、游艇码头、购物胜地、豪华酒店等世界级的城市设施和配套项目，规划建筑规模达5.73平方千米。科伦坡港口城一期填海造地投资约14亿美元，带动二期开发投资达130亿美元。

科伦坡港口城项目整体工期约25年，于2014年9月开工。在中斯双方的共同协作下，2021年5月斯里兰卡议会正式通过《科伦坡港口城经济委员会法案》，从立法层面赋予港口城经济特区的地位，并给予了一系列营商便利和税收优惠政策。

经过多年建设，科伦坡港口城从斯里兰卡人民的美好夙

Colombo Port City

Colombo Port City is a key BRI project implemented by China and Sri Lanka. Sri Lanka's largest foreign investment project, it is being developed by a Chinese company and the Sri Lankan government.

Located in Colombo's central business district, it will occupy 2.69 square kilometers of land reclaimed from the sea adjacent to the Port of Colombo. The whole city will have five functional zones: a financial district, a central park, an island for residence, a marina, and a zone of international brands. There will be office buildings, a medical center, schools, amusement facilities, a yacht marina, a shopping mall, and a luxury hotel.

The Port City will have a combined floor space of 5.73 square kilometers, with an initial investment of US$1.4 billion in land reclamation. It is expected to attract US$13 billion of further development investment.

Following the ground-breaking ceremony in September 2014, construction will continue for 25 years. Thanks to the coordination on both sides, the Sri Lankan parliament adopted the Colombo Port City Economic Commission Act in May 2021, which granted the Port City status as a special economic zone and a number of preferential policies for business and taxation.

Colombo Port City is growing from a vision on

愿变成一座从印度洋海平面崛起的新城雏形，项目也从建设期进入蓬勃发展的开发运营期。项目建成后可提供超20万个就业岗位，并容纳超过28万人工作和生活，被《福布斯》杂志列为“影响未来的五座新城”之一。

a blueprint into a new city by the Indian Ocean. Some projects have been completed and are already in operation. The whole initiative will create more than 200,000 jobs and provide work and accommodation for more than 280,000 people. Colombo Port City was selected as one of the "Five New Cities to Shake Up the Future" by *Forbes* magazine in 2018.

中欧班列

中欧班列作为畅通亚欧货物贸易的重要稳定通道，是共建“一带一路”的重要成果和突出亮点。2011年3月，自重庆出发的首趟中欧班列从新疆阿拉山口口岸出境，标志着铁路开始成为海运、空运之外连接亚欧大陆的第三条运输大道。此后，在“一带一路”倡议的推动下，中欧班列进入高速发展期。2015年3月中国发布的《推动共建丝绸之路经济带和21世纪海上丝绸之路的愿景与行动》明确将中欧班列建设列为国家发展重点。2016年6月，中国铁路正式启用“中欧班列”统一品牌。

近年来，中欧班列初步探索形成了多国协作的国际班列运行机制。中国、白俄罗斯、德国、哈萨克斯坦、蒙古、波兰和俄罗斯等7国铁路公司签署了《关于深化中欧班列合作协议》。如今，中欧班列通达欧洲25个国家的200多个城市，86条时速120千米的运行线路穿越亚欧腹地主要区域，

China Railway Express to Europe

The China Railway Express to Europe is an important and stable channel for trade in goods between Asia and Europe. It is a success story about the BRI.

The launch in March 2011 of a rail freight service from the Chinese city of Chongqing, via the Alashankou border crossing in Xinjiang, through Central Asia to Europe, ushered in a new era for rail freight as an alternative to shipping by sea or air. China-Europe rail cargo transport has subsequently gained rapid traction, fueled by the rollout of the BRI.

China's rail link to Europe was highlighted in the white paper published in March 2015, *Joining Hands to Build a Silk Road Economic Belt and a 21st Century Maritime Silk Road – Vision and Actions*. The name "China Railway Express" was formally introduced in June 2016, for all Europe-bound trains.

The operation of the China Railway Express trains has led to the creation of a multilateral coordination mechanism for international rail transport. To date, the railway companies of seven countries – China, Belarus, Germany, Kazakhstan, Mongolia, Poland and Russia – have signed cooperation agreements. The freight trains have reached more than 200 cities in 25 European countries, running on 86 rail lines at a speed of 120 kilometers per hour through

物流配送网络覆盖亚欧大陆，运输货物品类涉及服装鞋帽、汽车及配件、粮食、木材等53大门类5万多种品类。面对新冠肺炎疫情以及国际形势等影响，中欧班列充分发挥速度快、运能大、安全高效等优势，筑起了国际携手抗疫的“生命通道”。

中欧班列作为“铁轨上的‘一带一路’”，架起了中国与欧洲、世界联系的桥梁，推进了中国与沿线国家的互联互通，逐渐成为全球认可的中国物流名片。它不再只是一条条开放的线段，而是已形成一张开放的网络；它不仅发挥着货物运输通道的功能，而且将承担更多的使命：吸纳全球资金、资源、技术、人才等产业要素，发挥全球产业衔接功能。

the main regions of the Eurasian hinterland. The logistic distribution network covers the entire Eurasian continent, transporting more than 50,000 types of products in 53 categories such as garments, hats and shoes, automobiles and parts, grain, and timber.

In the face of the Covid-19 pandemic and international turmoil, these freight trains have fully displayed their strengths in fast and safe transport of large volumes of goods and ensured supplies for the global fight against the virus.

The China Railway Express service, seen as the "Belt and Road on rail," helps improve connectivity between China and Europe and the rest of the world, and is a prominent calling card for Chinese logistics services. An interconnected network has been formed by joining individual lines. In addition to offering freight transport solutions, it contributes to flows of global investment, resources, technology, and skilled personnel and facilitates global cross-sector collaboration.

雅万高速铁路

雅万高速铁路（简称“雅万高铁”）是一条连接印度尼西亚首都雅加达和第四大城市万隆之间的高速铁路，是“一带一路”倡议和“全球海洋支点”构想对接的重大标志性项目，全长142.3千米，最高设计时速350千米。2023年10月，雅万高铁正式启用，从雅加达至万隆的时间缩短为40分钟左右。

雅万高铁是中国高铁全系统、全要素、全生产链走出去的“第一单”，它采用中国铁路技术标准，按照当地的气候、线路条件、沿线群众文化传统和生活习惯为印尼“量身打造”。2015年10月，中国铁路总公司在雅加达与印度尼西亚四家国有企业签署协议，组建中国—印尼雅万高铁合资公司，负责印尼雅加达至万隆高速铁路项目的建设和运营。雅万高铁项目是国际上首个由政府主导搭台、两国企业间进行合作建设的高铁项目，是国际铁路合作模式的一次探索和创新。

雅万高铁作为印尼乃至东南亚的第一条高速铁路，对助力印尼经济社会发展、深化中印尼两国合作、促进共建“一

Jakarta-Bandung High-Speed Railway

The Jakarta-Bandung High-speed Railway is a 142-kilometer rail line linking Indonesia's capital Jakarta to Bandung, the fourth largest city in the country. It is a landmark project dovetailing China's BRI and Indonesia's Global Maritime Fulcrum strategy. With a designed speed of 350 kilometers per hour, the travel time between the two hubs has been cut to about 40 minutes after the railway came into operation in October 2023.

This was the first overseas high-speed rail system built by China utilizing Chinese technology, components, and industrial chains, with design considerations given to local climate and conditions, and the traditions and habits of the local residents.

An agreement was reached in October 2015 between China Railway Co. and four Indonesian state-owned enterprises to establish a Chinese-Indonesian consortium tasked to construct and operate the line. The project represents an innovative approach to international cooperation, with businesses from both countries involved under the sponsorship of the two governments.

The first high-speed rail project in Indonesia and all of Southeast Asia, it is expected to greatly boost local economic and social development, reinforce cooperation between China and Indonesia, and promote high-quality

带一路”高质量发展，具有十分重要的意义：不仅将直接拉动印尼冶炼、制造、基建、电力、物流等配套产业发展，增加就业机会，推动产业结构升级，而且在建成通车后，还将形成一个新的高铁经济走廊和涵盖周边、充满活力的双城经济体，便利当地民众出行，丰富人民生活，带动沿线旅游产业快速发展，并为中印尼之间在基础设施、商贸等领域的进一步合作奠定良好基础。

Belt and Road cooperation.

Supporting a high-speed rail economic corridor and a twin-city cluster, the rail link will stimulate growth in sectors such as metallurgy, manufacturing, infrastructure, power generation and logistics. It will create jobs and promote industrial structure upgrading in Indonesia. It will also facilitate travel and promote tourism along the line, and provide a sound base for further cooperation between China and Indonesia in infrastructure and trade.

亚的斯—阿达玛高速公路

亚的斯—阿达玛高速公路由中国政府融资支持，全部采用中国技术和标准承建，按双向6车道、时速120千米标准建设，是埃塞俄比亚第一条现代化高速公路，也是东非地区规模最大、等级最高的高速公路。该条公路连通埃塞俄比亚首都亚的斯亚贝巴和该国第二大城市阿达玛，公路通车后，从亚的斯亚贝巴到阿达玛的时间由2.5小时缩短为45分钟，对改善埃塞俄比亚民众出行、提高运输效率、吸引外商投资都发挥着重要作用。

亚的斯—阿达玛高速公路全长84千米，一期和二期项目分别于2014年5月和2016年8月竣工。项目实施中，承建的中国企业不仅雇用大量本地劳动力，也对埃塞俄比亚输出了技术和管理经验，有助于埃塞俄比亚加强基建能力建设。

Addis Ababa-Adama Expressway

The Addis Ababa-Adama Expressway was built with financing support from the Chinese government and using Chinese technology and standards.

With a designed speed of 120 kilometers per hour, the six-lane road is the first modern expressway in Ethiopia, and it is of the highest grade in East Africa. Connecting Ethiopia's capital Addis Ababa to its second largest city Adama, the expressway has shortened the travel time from 2.5 hours to 45 minutes. The project has facilitated travel, improved transport efficiency, and increased Ethiopia's ability to attract foreign investment.

The two phases of the construction of the 84-kilometer-long road were completed in May 2014 and August 2016. In addition to employing a large number of local workers, the Chinese contractor brought technical and managerial expertise to Ethiopia, helping the country expand its capability in infrastructure development.

卡洛特水电站

卡洛特水电站是“中巴经济走廊”能源合作优先实施项目和首个大型水电投资项目，位于巴基斯坦旁遮普省卡洛特地区，是杰赫勒姆河梯级水电规划的第四级。项目装机容量72万千瓦，采用“建设—拥有—运营—移交”（BOOT）方式开发，总投资约17.4亿美元。2022年6月，卡洛特水电站正式全面投入商业运营。运营期为30年，到期后无偿转让给巴基斯坦政府。

卡洛特水电站是“一带一路”建设的首个水电项目，也是丝路基金2014年年底注册成立后投资的首个项目，是迄今为止中国企业在海外投资在建的最大绿地水电项目。水电站每年可提供约32亿千瓦时的清洁电能，可满足当地500万人口用电需求，将为巴基斯坦经济社会发展提供可靠的能源支持。除主要用于发电外，该项目还有防洪、拦沙、改善下游航运条件和发展库区通航等综合效益。在建设高峰期，项目为当地提供数千个就业岗位，并带动当地电力配套行业的协调发展和产业升级。电站项目还有利于巴基斯坦获得

Karot Hydropower Plant

The Karot Hydropower Plant is the first large hydropower investment venture and a priority project of energy cooperation in the CPEC. It is located in Punjab province of Pakistan and is the fourth of five cascade hydropower stations planned on the Jhelum River. The project operates on a build-own-operate-transfer basis, with an investment of US$1.74 billion and an installed capacity of 720 megawatts. It started commercial operation in June 2022, and its ownership will be transferred to the Pakistani government at no cost in 30 years.

It was the first hydropower project implemented under the BRI and the first project financed by the Silk Road Fund since its inception in 2014. It is also the largest green field hydropower project undertaken overseas by a Chinese company to date.

The plant will generate 3.2 billion kilowatt-hours of clean electricity per year to meet the needs of 5 million local residents and provide reliable energy support for Pakistan's economic and social development.

In addition to power generation, it will help with flood prevention and sediment control and improve downstream and reservoir transport services. The project created several thousand jobs during the construction period, and has spurred coordinated and upgraded development in related

清洁、廉价、可持续的能源，预计每年可减少二氧化碳排放350万吨，有助于实现“中巴经济走廊”清洁和绿色愿景。

sectors. It will provide clean, cheap, and sustainable energy to Pakistan, reduce CO_2 emissions by 3.5 million tons per year, and contribute to the clean and green CPEC vision.

佩列沙茨大桥

佩列沙茨大桥是一座设计总长2440米的公路斜拉桥，横跨克罗地亚南部亚得里亚海的小斯通湾，连接克罗地亚陆地南段与佩列沙茨半岛。佩列沙茨大桥及其连接线一期工程项目于2018年1月由中国企业中标，并于当年开工。2022年7月，佩列沙茨大桥正式通车。

佩列沙茨大桥是中克共建“一带一路”和中国—中东欧国家合作的标志性项目，也是中方在克罗地亚承建的最大规模的基础设施项目。跨海大桥大大缩短通往克罗地亚南部的旅行时间，并对南部地区的交通、旅游和经济等产生重要影响。

佩列沙茨跨海大桥顺利通车为中克、中欧合作树立了新典范，将进一步深化中克政治互信，加强双方发展战略对接，扩大经贸等各领域合作，推动中克全面合作伙伴关系迈上新台阶。

Peljesac Bridge

This is a 2.4-kilometer cable-stayed bridge over the Mali Ston Bay of the Adriatic Sea, which connects Croatia's mainland with its territory on the Peljesac Peninsula. A Chinese company won the tender in January 2018 for the first phase of the bridge and its extension and started construction in the same year. The bridge opened to traffic in July 2022.

The bridge is a hallmark project of cooperation between China and Croatia under the BRI, and between China and Central and Eastern Europe, and the largest infrastructure project undertaken by China in Croatia. It has greatly shortened the travel time to southern Croatia and boosted transport, tourism, and the economy in the southern region.

The bridge's completion has set a good example for bilateral cooperation, and will increase mutual political trust, further synergize the development strategies of the two countries, expand economic and trade cooperation, and raise the bilateral comprehensive cooperative partnership to a new level.

中埃苏伊士经贸合作区

中埃苏伊士经贸合作区是中国参与开发建设的重点境外经贸合作区，自2008年开始建设。

合作区位于“一带一路”和“苏伊士运河走廊经济带”交汇点上，地处亚、非、欧三大洲交界的金三角地带，地理位置优越，是埃及当前唯一完成全方位配套的、可供企业直接入驻的工业园区，已形成石油装备、高低压电器、纺织服装、新型建材、机械制造五大产业园区，并带动上、下游产业入区，快速形成产业集群效应。

2014年9月，中埃双方签订了合作区扩展区项目，扩展区面积6平方千米，将分三期开发，开发建设总投资约2.3亿美元。2016年1月，习近平在访问埃及期间，与埃及总统塞西共同为扩展区揭牌。

截至2023年7月，合作区共吸引140余家企业入驻，实

China-Egypt Suez Economic and Trade Cooperation Zone

The China-Egypt Suez Economic and Trade Cooperation Zone is one of the key overseas economic and trade cooperation zones supported by the Chinese government.

Construction on the zone started in 2008, which is located in the triangle between Asia, Africa, and Europe, a region where the Belt and Road routes join Egypt's Suez Canal Corridor Economic Zone. Enjoying a convenient location, it is the only industrial park in Egypt with complete facilities, where businesses can move in at any time.

There are five industrial parks for different businesses: petroleum equipment manufacturing, high and low voltage electric equipment, textiles and garments, new building materials, and machinery manufacturing. Upstream and downstream industries have been attracted to produce industrial clusters.

In September 2014 China and Egypt agreed to expand the zone by 6 square kilometers, which would be developed in three phases with a total investment of US$230 million. During his visit to Egypt in January 2016, Xi Jinping unveiled the expansion zone together with Egyptian President Abdel-Fattah al-Sisi.

By July 2023, more than 140 enterprises had settled

际投资额超16亿美元，累计销售额超37亿美元，缴纳税费超2亿美元，直接提供近6000个就业岗位，产业带动就业约5万人。巨石、西电、大运、美的等多家行业龙头企业，以及埃及、阿联酋、加拿大等国家和地区的国际企业入驻。合作区逐渐成为“一带一路”沿线重要的国际经贸合作平台。

在埃及“苏伊士运河走廊开发计划”和共建“一带一路”倡议的推动下，合作区持续发展，在红海之滨的荒滩上建起一座现代化产业新城，成为中埃合作的重要成果。

in the zone, bringing over US$1.6 billion of agreed investment. Total sales exceeded US$3.7 billion and taxes US$200 million, and nearly 6,000 direct jobs and about 50,000 indirect jobs have been created. Flagship Chinese companies such as Jushi, XD Group, Dayun Group, and Midea, and international enterprises from Egypt, the United Arab Emirates, and Canada have moved in. The zone has now grown into an important platform for international economic and trade cooperation along the Belt and Road routes.

Promoted by the Egyptian Suez Canal Corridor Project and the BRI, a modern industrial city is blossoming on a once-barren beach by the Red Sea, showcasing Sino-Egyptian cooperation.

中国—上海合作组织地方经贸合作示范区

2018年6月，习近平在上合组织成员国元首理事会第十八次会议上宣布，“中国政府支持在青岛建设中国—上海合作组织地方经贸合作示范区”。

中国—上合组织地方经贸合作示范区辖域总面积约108平方千米，包括核心区和3个片区。自2018年以来，上合示范区积极推进上合组织和“一带一路”沿线国家地方经贸合作，开行中欧班列超3000列，通达上合组织和“一带一路”沿线23个国家50多个城市，集聚贸易主体2000余家。

上合示范区启动建设以来，全力推进国际物流、现代贸易、双向投资合作、商旅文交流发展“四个中心”和上合组织经贸学院建设，为国际双多边框架下地方经贸合作提供场景、模式和范例。有关各方通过上合示范区参与共建“一带一路”，有利于布局国内国际两个市场，打通内外联通的战略大走廊，带动区域经济发展走向更加开放包容的新格局。

China-SCO Local Economic and Trade Cooperation Demonstration Zone

Xi Jinping announced at the 18th meeting of the Council of Heads of Member States of the SCO, held in the Chinese city of Qingdao in June 2018, that China would support building a demonstration zone in Qingdao for China-SCO local economic and trade cooperation.

The demonstration zone occupies 108 square kilometers, including one core zone and three supplementary districts. Since 2018, the zone has been dedicated to economic and trade cooperation among SCO countries and among the countries along the Belt and Road routes. More than 3,000 freight trains have traveled between Qingdao and 50-plus cities in 23 countries along the Belt and Road routes, including SCO member states, and more than 2,000 trade entities are operating inside the zone.

Great efforts have been made to develop the four centers for international logistics, modern trade, two-way investment, and business, tourism and cultural exchanges, and the China-SCO Institute of Economy and Trade. They have provided scenarios, models, and examples for bilateral and multilateral cooperation. The zone has helped relevant parties join Belt and Road cooperation, plan their domestic and overseas markets, and open new ground for open and inclusive development of the local economy.

“小而美”项目

在第三次“一带一路”建设座谈会上，习近平指出，小而美的项目，是直接影响到民众的。今后要将小而美项目作为对外合作的优先事项，加强统筹谋划，发挥援外资金四两拨千斤作用，形成更多接地气、聚人心的项目。

事实上，在对外开放过程中，中国不仅推进了许多“高大上”的国际项目，也参与了不少“小而美”的民生工程。例如，20世纪80年代以来，为了兼顾扶贫与环保，中国形成了特有的“以草代木”栽培食药用菌的菌草技术。菌草技术现已推广到世界上百个国家和地区，成为造福广大发展中国家的“幸福草”，为广大发展中国家脱贫致富、实现可持续发展开辟了新的发展道路。

一批“小而美”的农业、医疗、减贫等民生项目相继落地，有效地提升了相关国家民生水平，推动实现中国与共建“一带一路”国家人民“心联通”。

"Small Yet Smart" Projects

At a domestic meeting on Belt and Road cooperation held in November 2021, Xi Jinping said that as "small yet smart" projects often bring direct benefits to the people, they should be a priority in China's cooperation with other countries in the future. Well-designed plans are needed to make the best of outbound investment to benefit the people and meet their needs.

China has invested in many large international projects and also participated in numerous "small yet smart" projects related to people's daily needs. One example is its introduction of a technology based on a fungi-grass, called *juncao* in Chinese. Substituting grass for wood to breed edible and medicinal fungi, the technology has been widely applied since the 1980s in China and supports both poverty reduction and environmental protection. To date, the technology has been introduced to over 100 countries and regions, and the "grass of happiness," as *juncao* is nicknamed, now helps developing countries eliminate poverty and achieve sustainable development.

Other "small yet smart" projects implemented in farming, medical services, and poverty reduction have also effectively improved local people's lives and built closer friendships between China and other BRI countries.

图书在版编目（CIP）数据

中国关键词．“一带一路”篇：汉英对照 / 中国外文出版发行事业局，当代中国与世界研究院，中国翻译研究院著；韩清月，蔡力坚译．-- 3 版．-- 北京：新世界出版社，2023.10

ISBN 978-7-5104-7745-4

Ⅰ．①中… Ⅱ．①中… ②当… ③中… ④韩… ⑤蔡… Ⅲ．①中国特色社会主义 - 社会主义建设模式 - 研究 - 汉、英②“一带一路” - 国际合作 - 研究 - 汉、英 Ⅳ．① D616 ② F125.5

中国国家版本馆 CIP 数据核字 (2023) 第 179817 号

中国关键词：“一带一路”篇 第 3 版
（汉英对照）

作　　者：中国外文出版发行事业局　当代中国与世界研究院
　　　　　中国翻译研究院
翻　　译：韩清月　蔡力坚
审　　定：徐明强
改　　稿：David Ferguson［英］
项目统筹：申　阳
项目执行：华光灿
责任编辑：赵如意
责任校对：宣　慧　张杰楠
责任印制：王宝根
出　　版：新世界出版社
网　　址：http://www.nwp.com.cn
社　　址：北京西城区百万庄大街 24 号（100037）
发 行 部：(010)6899 5968（电话）(010)6899 0635（电话）
总 编 室：(010)6899 5424（电话）(010)6832 6679（传真）
版 权 部：+8610 6899 6306（电话） nwpcd@sina.com（电邮）
印　　刷：天津中印联印务有限公司
经　　销：新华书店
开　　本：880mm×1230mm　1/32　　尺　　寸：120mm×200mm
字　　数：120 千字　　印　　张：6.25
版　　次：2017 年 5 月第 1 版　2019 年 4 月第 2 版　2023 年 10 月第 3 版
印　　次：2023 年 10 月第 3 版第 1 次印刷，累计第 7 次印刷
书　　号：ISBN 978-7-5104-7745-4
定　　价：68.00 元